Praise f

"This book, written in a ~~company feminine~~ voice that is supportive, authoritative, and most caring, mandates recovery as a prerequisite for genuine spiritual insight and freedom from addiction. Laura Burges's personal voice is a pleasure to hear."
—Sylvia Boorstein, cofounder of Spirit Rock Meditation Center and author of *Pay Attention for Goodness' Sake*

"*The Zen Way of Recovery* is a gentle and wise primer to Buddhism written by one who has used the practices to heal herself of addiction. The lessons learned are shared with humility and compassion and in no way minimize or sugar coat the difficulties we all face as vulnerable human beings prone to suffer. An excellent book that will be of help to many."
—Dr. Fred Luskin, director of the Stanford University Forgiveness Project and author of *Forgive for Good: A Proven Prescription for Health and Happiness*

"This wonderful, friendly, helpful book weds the warm, practical humanity of the recovery community with the gem-like clarity and deep, ancient practices of Zen Buddhism. If you are in recovery and seeking to explore a more structured spiritual path or are secretly struggling with an addiction that your religious life hasn't 'cured,' I can think of no more trustworthy guide than Zen teacher Laura Burges. She has walked the walk for decades, with kindness, deep knowledge, and gentle humor. There is no inherent conflict between Buddhist teachings and the spiritual path of recovery. Laura shines a light on how the practices and teachings of each can support the other."
—Katy Butler, author of *Knocking on Heaven's Door* and *The Art of Dying Well*

# *The* Zen Way *of* RECOVERY

## AN ILLUMINATED PATH OUT OF THE DARKNESS OF ADDICTION

### LAURA BURGES

SHAMBHALA

Shambhala Publications, Inc.
2129 13th Street
Boulder, Colorado 80302
www.shambhala.com

Cover art: cheng feng/Unsplash
Cover design: Katrina Noble
Interior design: Katrina Noble

Excerpts from *When Things Fall Apart* by Pema Chödrön, © 1997. Reprinted by arrangement with Shambhala Publications, Inc., Boulder, CO.

9 8 7 6 5 4 3 2 1

First Edition
Printed in the United States of America

Shambhala Publications makes every effort to print on acid-free, recycled paper. Shambhala Publications is distributed worldwide by Penguin Random House, Inc., and its subsidiaries.

LIBRARY OF CONGRESS CATALOGING-IN-PUBLICATION DATA
Names: Burges, Laura, author.
Title: The Zen way of recovery: an illuminated path out of the darkness of
    addiction / Laura Burges.
Description: Boulder: Shambhala, 2023.
Identifiers: LCCN 2022032542 | ISBN 9781645471202 (trade paperback)
Subjects: LCSH: Drugs—Religious aspects—Buddhism. | Drug addiction—
    Treatment—Religious aspects—Buddhism. | Substance abuse—Religious
    aspects—Buddhism. | Compulsive behavior—Religious aspects—
    Buddhism. | Habit breaking—Religious aspects—Buddhism.
Classification: LCC BQ4570.D78 B87 2023 | DDC 294.3/442—dc23/eng/20220713
LC record available at https://lccn.loc.gov/2022032542

*This book is dedicated*
*to all those on the path of recovery,*
*past, present, and future.*
*May we continue to heal with one another,*
*one step at a time.*

May all the Buddhas and Ancestors
   who have attained the Buddha Way
   be compassionate to us and free us from karmic effects,
   allowing us to practice The Way without hindrance.

—Dogen Zenji

# CONTENTS

# THE ZEN WAY
# OF RECOVERY

# INTRODUCTION

I vow to live and be lived for the benefit of all beings.
—The Bodhisattva Vow

Buddhism did not cure my alcoholism. I turned to Zen to change my life, to align myself with the sangha (the community of Buddhist practitioners), and to find relief from the suffering of addiction. But until I opened my heart to the principles of recovery, I was cut off from the deepest source of my own being. Now I find that Zen Buddhist practice, lived in accord with the solace of recovery, can offer a life that is full of possibilities.

It is understandable that those of us who are prone to addiction turn to drugs and alcohol and other distracting behaviors to medicate the distress within. I began drinking when I was a teenager, and alcohol promised to give me things I didn't have—self-confidence, an antidote to my social anxiety, and an ecstatic "yes" to a wide and wild life. Drugs and alcohol may be the closest thing to a spiritual experience that isn't.

Over time, addiction pulled me into a downward spiral, taking away all the things it had seemed to promise in the beginning—freedom, expansiveness, peace, relief. Discouraged but feeling that there might be another way, I stopped drinking and stepped onto the path of practice. At first, Zen helped me turn away from addiction and toward the sangha and a vital way of life. But ultimately, alcohol began to creep back into my life, and I knew that I needed to address the roots of this disease in a more direct and dynamic way. At the end of my drinking, I thought of all the gifted Buddhist teachers who could sit still for days at a time and shower us with illuminating dharma talks but, because they were powerless over their own addictive behavior, harmed their students and destroyed or deeply damaged their communities.

In this book, I share the teachings that have been helpful to me in my own recovery. But it is not meant to take the place of a program of recovery. If you struggle with addiction, you may experience craving for a substance or an addictive behavior once you start. You might notice that your personality changes when you use or act out. You may be having blackouts—memory lapses—as a result of using. You may be frustrated by the fact that you keep using despite negative consequences. Maybe you have tried to stop and haven't been able to. You may have been discouraged to return to your addiction again and again despite periods of abstinence. Maybe the people who care about you have tried to tell you about their concerns. Do you lie about your use of substances or food, your sexual behavior, your gambling habit? Do you reveal one side of yourself to one group of people and a very different side to others? Do you lie to family or friends about the addictive behavior of someone you care for? Do you often put your own welfare aside in favor of focusing on someone you love and their struggles with addiction?

If any of these signs sound familiar to you, I strongly recommend that you find a recovery program that can directly address your addictive patterns rather than relying solely on Buddhist teachings to keep you sober. There, you can do the work that will help prepare you to fully engage in Zen practice. You can learn much from those who have made the journey through recovery ahead of you, even from people who may seem very different from you. Together, the paths of practice and of recovery can provide us with a wonderful strength that has previously been beyond our reach: the strength of fellowship and of sangha, the down-to-earth language and tools of recovery, and the wondrous teachings of the Buddha. In our recovery community, our collective intention to stay sober and help others gives us a profound power we never knew we had, including full participation in practice and the life of the sangha.

To be inclusive, I use the word *addiction* to refer to substances, including alcohol; to self-sabotaging or addictive behavior, such as sex and love addiction, gambling, screen addiction, workaholism, and issues around food; and to the addictive patterns of those you love. For me, the combined practices of Zen and recovery have offered a shining light to lead me out of the darkness of addiction

If you don't have access to a Buddhist sangha, I hope you will make a place for zazen (sitting meditation) in your life. You can read some simple instructions in the second chapter of this book to help you get started. There is a booklist in the back of the book to further your exploration of the intersection of practice and recovery.

Learning about Zen, we come upon the word *emptiness*. This word doesn't tell us that life is meaningless. One aspect of emptiness, from a Zen Buddhist point of view, is that we, and all things, are empty of a separate self. It is the marvelous realization that none of us exists as a solitary, isolated being. None of us, and nothing in this world, can exist for one nanosecond outside the causes and conditions that give rise to this moment. I am the sun, the stars, the rain, the earth, and the fruits of the earth. I am a vast collection of elements beyond the small self with which I tend to identify. I am my parents, and their parents, and their parents. I am everyone who has taught me and everyone whom I have taught. Every encounter of my life, every moment of my life, has contributed to who I am today.

Many of us have tried, in desperation, to control our addictions by ourselves. We conducted these experiments in lonely solitude, and for the most part, our efforts have been futile. When we step into the sunlight of recovery, we find that we can tap into the boundless energy, optimism, and hope of others, and not just among the people we meet today; we also benefit from the efforts of countless beings stretching back into timelessness. Our effort will, in turn, benefit countless others. We are not alone. Recovery, like Buddhism, is passed from warm hand to warm hand, and it is in offering help to others that we are healed.

This book reflects my own experience and understanding of Zen practice and recovery, and I take responsibility for any errors or omissions. I don't share these teachings because I've mastered them—that might take many lifetimes. As the Vipassana teacher Jack Kornfield once put it, "If you can sit quietly after difficult news, if in financial downturns you remain perfectly calm, if you can see your neighbors travel to fantastic places without a twinge of jealousy, if you can happily eat whatever is put on your plate, . . . if you can always find contentment just where you are, you are probably a dog."

This book isn't meant to be a survey of all Zen Buddhism. My intention is to share my understanding of some practical dharma teachings—as well as teachings beyond Buddhism—that, along with my recovery program, have helped me to navigate everyday life without the use of drugs or alcohol or other self-destructive behaviors. While my autobiographical information is accurate to the best of my memory, some of the names of the people in these pages have been changed to protect their anonymity or because they are no longer able to give me permission to use their identities.

Practice and recovery open us to the Bodhisattva Vow, the intention to live and be lived for the benefit of all beings. In the broadest sense, anyone who seeks awakening, anyone who directs their life toward this vow, could be called a bodhisattva. Let's not call ourselves bodhisattvas, though. Let's just humbly walk this path together, one step at time. I hope this book will help you find your way.

## Reflections and Practices

You will find some suggested reflections and practices at the end of each chapter. You can enlist these to spark thoughts, realizations, and memories; you can write them down and/or share them with a trusted friend. Writing, because it is a mind/body activity, tends to help us go deeper and uncover thoughts and feelings that we didn't know we had. You might want to have a journal on hand to record your responses:

- Have you ever tried to stop using or acting out and found that it was difficult to do so?
- Has anyone commented on the effect your addictive behavior has on them? How did you respond?

- Do you lie to others about your behavior or the behavior of others, and are you frequently making excuses for yourself or for them?
- Do you persist in addictive behavior despite repeated negative results?
- What does your addictive behavior seem to give you? What has it taken away?
- Make a list of what troubles you about your addictive patterns.

IMPORTANT:
- Please be aware that trauma is often at the root of addiction. If this is part of your story, treatment designed to address it will be important.
- Depending on your situation, and the nature of your addiction, it can be dangerous and difficult to detox on your own. It will be wise to seek medical advice to assess whether a supervised detox is best for you.

# 1

## Way Seeking Mind

> To believe means to have faith that one is already inherently in
> The Way, and that one is not lost, deluded or upside down, and
> no increase, and no decrease, and no mistake.
>
> —Dogen Zenji

I HAVE PRACTICED for many years at San Francisco Zen Center,
part of the Soto Zen lineage from Japan, and these are the words
of our great Soto Zen ancestor Dogen Zenji. I first read them on
the refrigerator of my lifelong friend Deborah. We had grown up
together in Pleasant Hill, California, and had been best friends
as children, riding horses together over the rolling hills of Con-
tra Costa County, but we had lost track of one another. I ran into
her in Davis when I was about twenty-four. Deborah had read *Zen
Mind, Beginner's Mind*, the Zen classic by Shunryu Suzuki Roshi,
founder of Zen Center, and she was sitting zazen with a local
group of practitioners. In Deborah's kitchen, talking late into the

night, we shared our first impressions of Buddhism and the various insults and joys that life had dealt us since we'd seen each other last.

It was a time in my life when I was totally lost, deluded, and upside down. I wondered how I could ever believe otherwise. Dependence on alcohol and the wreckage it had caused had left me without hope. I had spent a year living in Alaska and returned to San Francisco in a state of profound demoralization. Shortly after that late-night conversation with my friend, learning about sangha and Zen practice, I found myself standing at the doors of San Francisco Zen Center.

Not many people wake up one morning and say, "It's a beautiful day. I think I'll go sit cross-legged facing a wall for the rest of my life." Most of us have come face-to-face with the First Noble Truth by the time we step onto the path of practice, the truth that in life there is great suffering. Catching a glimpse of Buddhism, I thought that perhaps the teachings of Zen could help release me from my own self-destructive way of living, from the suffering I had caused myself and others. This was the opening of Way Seeking Mind, stepping onto the path of awakening.

The source of suffering is one of the elemental questions of human life. When my daughter, Nova, was about eight, I was tucking her in one night, and she asked me, "Mommy, why are people born to suffer and die?"

I replied, "Well, that's a question that human beings have asked since the beginning of time."

She thought for a moment and said, "You know, that doesn't really help."

It startled me to hear my little girl ask me her question, but it made me remember that I had wondered, when I was little, why we are all here. I remember thinking that we must be here to help each other—but that didn't make sense, because if we *weren't* here, then there would be nobody here to help.

My friend Robyn and I often had sleepovers, camping out in the backyard. What did we talk about into the wee hours of the morning? What made us laugh so long and so hard? I don't remember. But we forged a friendship that has lasted our whole lives. One Saturday morning, when I was twelve, I woke up in my sleeping bag in Robyn's backyard and looked up at pots of geraniums on a blue wall. Suddenly, it was as if a veil had been lifted, and I saw a radiant world before me. I didn't really know how to put this into words, and I didn't tell anyone else about it, but I thought of it as "the day I woke up."

Robyn was Catholic, and I would sometimes go to Mass with her and wonder at the statues with their sad eyes and their chests open to reveal burning hearts, pierced by arrows. I was intrigued with the notion of confession, that you could pretty much do whatever you wanted as long as you told a priest about it and said you were sorry. While Catholicism wasn't for me, there was something compelling about the mysterious rituals, the Latin incantations, those tortured but beatific statues, and the smell of incense. Robyn would receive a communion host, but I wasn't allowed to because I wasn't Catholic. In the Protestant churches my family went to, communion was little cubes of Wonder Bread and Welch's grape juice.

I was in eighth grade when I was rocked, as was our entire country, by the assassination of President John F. Kennedy. This was followed by other murders—Dr. Martin Luther King Jr., Robert Kennedy, Malcolm X, Medgar Evers, and many others. I watched the Vietnam War on television and saw countless coffins coming home, draped in American flags. I saw a Buddhist monk, Thich Quang Duc, immolate himself in front of a temple, sitting upright, legs crossed in full lotus, engulfed in flames. I saw American college students and protesters in Chicago being attacked by the police who were supposed to protect us.

Everything I believed in and counted on was being pulled out from under me. People my age, many of whom went on to use drugs and alcohol and the path of excess, were deeply affected by the cumulative effect of these cataclysmic reversals. We had grown up with promises of an elusive "American Dream," while we were subject to regular air-raid drills, diving under our wobbly wooden desks at school to practice hiding from nuclear bombs— as if that would help. I wonder now if we weren't suffering from a kind of collective form of post-traumatic stress disorder that we treated with drugs and alcohol. Each of us is also a conduit that contains the "ancient, twisted karma" of our own family history.

But we, as a generation, also began to question the "truths" that we had grown up with. Many of us were on the front lines of protests that gave birth to the civil rights movement, to women's rights and gay liberation, and to an end of the Vietnam War.

While my family wasn't strongly religious, we went to church every Sunday. After sampling various Protestant churches, my folks settled on the Unitarian Church, which seemed to me to be the next best thing to not having to go to church at all. When I moved on to Friends Meeting, I loved sitting with others in silence, and I liked that there was no altar or cross or even a minister. Quakers believe that you don't need an intermediary to commune with a higher power, that there is a divine spark within each of us. Both the Unitarians and the Quakers address the horrors of war and work actively against that horror, and I understood the integrity of peace work as a religious imperative, a practical application of respect for life on our planet.

When I was a teenager, my mom gave me Alan Watts's *The Book: On the Taboo Against Knowing Who You Are*, the first book I ever read about Buddhism, and that led me to *Siddhartha* by Hermann Hesse. I can't find this exchange in Hesse's book so I must have imagined that, when Siddhartha went to his father to ask if he could leave home and become an ascetic, his father refused, and then Siddhartha said, "I can wait, I can fast, and I can pray." So he waited and fasted and prayed until his father gave him his blessing.

One night, when I was about seventeen, I came home late, in the early hours of the morning, after going to San Francisco with my boyfriend, Sam. I opened the front door quietly and tiptoed across the dark living room. Suddenly a light was switched on. My mother was sitting on the couch. She grounded me, and I, of course, thought this was a great offense to my personal sovereignty. The next day, I sat under the walnut tree in the backyard all day long and thought, "I can wait, I can fast, and I can pray." I'm sure that I kept looking at the kitchen window to see if my mom was gazing out at me with a look of admiration or alarm. I hoped that she might come out and ask what on earth I was doing, so that I could reply, "I can wait, I can fast, and I can pray." She didn't.

I encountered drugs and alcohol, and they quickly became a shortcut to what I thought was a spiritual experience. When I drank, I felt the painful boundaries between me and other people melt away. To me, this was freedom, the freedom to do and be whatever I wanted, without thought of the consequences. In another favorite Hermann Hesse book, *Demian*, I found these incantatory words: "The bird fights its way out of the egg. The egg is the world. Who would be born must first destroy a world." I thought this was wonderful. I was going to fight my way out of the egg and destroy a world!

Sam got us some Hawaiian baby woodrose, a seedpod with psychedelic properties that you could buy at plant nurseries. One night at his house, we ate some by the handful as if they were sunflower seeds. I got very, very high. We were laughing hysterically, rolling around on the floor, when his parents came home unexpectedly, and Sam quickly got me into the car, dropped me off in front of my house, and drove away.

When I walked in the front door, my sister Betsy was ironing in the living room, her hair in braids. I felt I was looking through a thick pane of glass, that Betsy still existed in ordinary reality and I was forever outside that reality, never to return. I went to my room and got into bed. "The bird fights its way out of the egg," I was chanting. "The egg is the world. Who would be born must first destroy a world . . ." My mother's voice cut through this reverie, and she hustled me into the shower, assuming I was drunk. My brother Peter, though, thought that I must be on acid, and I could hear him saying, "She's tripping, Mom! Be cool!"

I was shut up in my room and descended into a tortured realm of nightmare. The next day, I woke up after little sleep and stepped back into that ordinary reality that I had longed for the night before. But the hellish visions that had visited me during that dark night haunted me for a long time. By comparison, alcohol seemed like a warm and familiar friend.

Early in my drinking, I had what I learned later are some of the symptoms of alcoholism: craving, a high tolerance for alcohol, personality change, and blackouts. Once I started drinking, I craved more. I was proud that I could drink others under the table. When I drank, my personality changed, and I said and did things I would never have done had I not been drinking. And I began to black out, to have memory lapses. I would wake up in the morning not remembering what I had done the night before. Though it terrified me that I could be out in the world, unaware of what I was doing, susceptible to danger, I wasn't ready to admit I had a problem. So that I could stay in denial, I compared myself only to people who drank even more than I did.

I broke up with Sam and started college and got back together with Sam and dropped out of college and went to work for a year to earn money so I could hit the road with Sam. With backpacks, we took nearly a year traveling overland from Europe to India. On the island of Crete, we took acid and floated through the orange groves by the light of the full moon. We took a train across Turkey and wandered deep into the Mideast, experiencing cultures permeated with religious practice. We saw camel trains plodding through the dusty streets of Herat, Afghanistan, bells tinkling, and had delicious dreams on brightly woven carpets at the opium den we discovered in the Old City one night. We drank when we could get alcohol, which was scarce in Muslim countries, and smoked hashish whenever we found it. We heard the frequent calls to prayer from the minarets. The Afghani women were curious about this Western girl in blue jeans and would shyly fold up the front of their burkas so I could see their faces. A young woman sitting in front of me on a bus offered me a stick of Wrigley's spearmint gum, smiling at me with her kohl-rimmed brown eyes. We passed through the towering mountains of the Hindu Kush and alongside silkworm farms in the mountains of Kashmir. We lived on a houseboat on Dal Lake in Srinagar, watching kingfishers swoop over the water. We saw people living and dying on the streets in India, and we saw *sadhus* practicing yoga along the side of the road.

When we came back, we were living in Pacific Grove and studying at Monterey Peninsula College when Sam's brother Chris told us about a place called Tassajara Zen Mountain Center, the first Buddhist monastery in America. Chris had been driving alone in his truck in the Los Padres National Forest. He was drunk, and he knew that he was running out of gas, but he figured he'd come to a town eventually. He drove the dusty, rutted road over the mountains and down into a deep and distant valley. He came at last to the gates of Tassajara. It was late at night. He was siphoning gas out of a car that was parked in front of the monastery when a monk appeared at his side.

The monk said, "Would you like to buy some gas?"

He invited Chris in, fed him, and let him use the legendary hot springs, giving him a loaf of freshly baked bread to take along on his ride home. Chris paid for the gas he'd stolen and headed back up the road.

This encounter had a profound effect on Chris. He was touched to be treated in this way when he was behaving badly. When we heard this story, we made a pilgrimage to Tassajara one hot summer day and spent the day skinny-dipping and drinking wine at the Narrows, the swimming hole downstream from the monastery. I didn't realize that within three years, I'd be living there as a Zen student myself.

Something deep inside me, some instinct for self-preservation, led me away from my troubled relationship with Sam. I knew that I needed to get as far away as I could from the wildness and the wildly excessive drinking we did together. We had met young people from Alaska who came to Monterey to study Russian at the language school there. My friend Sybil had suggested that I come north during the summer and work in the salmon canneries in Juneau, Alaska. I dropped out of school again and got a ride to Washington State to catch a ferry up the inland passage to Juneau, where I lived in a tent on a platform I built in the woods. Since they were only hiring residents in the canneries, I cleaned houses for a time and then got a job in the Alaska State Legislature, working for the senate majority leader, Jalmar Kerttula. I had great adventures with my friends, hiring a small plane and a pilot to explore the lakes and outposts nearby. But most nights, I was at the Dreamland or the Red Dog Saloon.

I once heard someone say, "I took a train, but my alcoholism took a plane." Though I had blamed the excesses of my drinking on Sam, I came face-to-face with my own insatiable thirst for alcohol. As winter came on, I moved to a small attic apartment in town and descended into a dark and frightening place. Alcohol, at the beginning, had given me things I didn't think I had, and now, one by one, it was taking them away. It led to a frigid isolation, a stagnant pool of self.

I had many moments of clarity during my time in Alaska, long before I stepped into the rooms of recovery. One morning, I was cleaning someone's house and picked up a newspaper. Dear Abby had written a column about alcoholism, including the 20 Questions, answers to which might indicate you have a drinking problem.* I was twenty-three, and I answered yes to

* NOTE: This list of questions was developed at Johns Hopkins University Hospital in the 1930s by Dr. Robert Seliger as a self-assessment for the alcoholic. Johns Hopkins no longer uses this particular assessment and suggests instead the twenty-five questions on the Michigan Alcohol Screening Test, which can be accessed online.

many of those questions. I didn't give this much thought at the time.

I remember walking through town with Sybil and asking her, "What did I do last night? The last thing I remember is going up on the stage at the Red Dog and taking the microphone away from the lead singer."

Sybil stopped in her tracks and stared at me. "I have never had so much to drink that I didn't remember what I did the night before," she said.

This was a revelation to me. I thought that happened to everyone, that everyone who drank had these kinds of lapses.

One afternoon, I was walking along the sidewalk, and I peered into a darkened bar. Inside, Indigenous women sat on stools, their heads down on the bar, passed out. An unbidden voice inside me said, "You're like that." I shook off that voice and walked on. Then one night, after drinking for hours with friends at the Dreamland, I came out of a blackout crawling through the snow. People die that way in Alaska. That finally got my attention.

It was clear that I needed to find another way to live.

I returned to San Francisco and finally graduated from college. I always thought I could quit drinking whenever I wanted to, and it was a rude awakening to find out I had some more demoralizing episodes ahead of me.

This was about the time that I ran into Deborah, and soon I found myself at Zen Center. I had some idea that when I knocked on that door, a black-robed monk would open it and ask me, "What is the sound of one hand clapping?" and that if I couldn't answer, he wouldn't let me in. That didn't happen.

I abruptly stopped drinking and gave up my apartment and my job at the Biofeedback Institute, where I trained clients to use biofeedback for relaxation. I moved into Zen Center and plunged headfirst into practice. I got to be friends with Issan Dorsey. He had become a Zen priest after a career performing as a female impersonator ("Tommy Dorsey, the Boy Who Looks Like the Girl Next Door") and then working as a community activist. Edward Espe Brown—author of *The Tassajara Bread Book* and many others—was *tanto* (head of practice) at City Center at the time, and he was clearly practicing with strong emotions. I thought that if they could practice, perhaps I too could take up this ancient way of life and be healed.

Without alcohol to numb me, a lot of pain—waves of loss, rage, shame, regret, and disappointment—came up for me when I began meditating in the *zendo* (meditation hall) with others. For a while, every time I sat on the *zafu* (a round, black meditation cushion), I cried silent tears. A friend of mine, who is not an alcoholic, put it so well: "Alcohol is like a credit card for pain. You pay it back later, with interest." My tears were like a quiet rain after a long dry season in hell.

Before too long, I was at Tassajara for the winter practice period, and as we say in Zen, I practiced "as if to save my head from fire." I remember my first Buddhist teacher, Zentatsu Richard Baker, standing behind me as I sat facing the wall during *sesshin* (a seven-day meditation retreat). He pounded his staff on the floor and intoned, "No mystic cry or special experience can help you until you have the great matter of your own life constantly before you and in the hands of your doing." Indeed.

I loved the rigor of life at Tassajara. I loved the order and ritual of practice, the intensity of cold in the winter, and the intentional activity of "chopping wood, carrying water." I loved the temple bells and the sound of the wooden hammer hitting the wooden *han* that echoed through the remote mountain valley, calling us to the meditation hall. I loved getting out of bed in my little cabin in the chill, dark morning to put on my robes and walk to the zendo. I loved the clarity that came with this radical shift in my life. There was a sense of timelessness in the mountain monastery, a chance to step out of American culture and find myself anew. I found a kind of freedom in *not* having to do whatever I wanted. The freedom of restraint. Being free to sit still. Being free *not* to do the first thing that came to mind. Freedom from drugs and alcohol. Being able to align myself with an ancient and timeless way of life. I no longer felt like a dry leaf in a strong wind.

I met my husband at Tassajara. We were married there and later returned to San Francisco to practice at City Center. When I held our newborn daughter, Nova—our one bright, shining pearl of a girl—in my arms, I understood that this life isn't just our own. It belongs, too, to the myriad beings that come before and after us. To squander a life is a kind of theft. We must live as fully as possible to honor this gift of human life. Later, our marriage ended, and I continued to raise my daughter with the help of many dear friends—especially Nova's loving godmother, Linda—and my family.

After I had been practicing for five years, someone offered me a drink and I took it. The years at Tassajara, the many hours of zazen, the wonderful teachings and teachers—none of them protected me from that first drink. For the next five years, I drank off and on, going for long periods without it but always coming back, mystified as to why I couldn't stop. I knew of gifted Buddhist teachers who had not been able to control their addictions and that the impact on their lives and on their communities had been devastating. Some had died because of addiction. I realized that, for me, Buddhism could not cure this disease.

Finally, I had to concede to my inmost self that I could not control my drinking. It was September, and I had gone back to school to work toward my teaching credential. I found myself sitting in a classroom, shaking and sick from the night before, and I heard a voice inside me call out from the depths of my being, "Please, please help me." Though I didn't know who or what was calling, I got up in the middle of that class and made a phone call that would profoundly change the trajectory of my life. I found a program of recovery and began to heal from the ancient, twisted karma of alcoholism.

I don't believe that moments of awakening are as rare as we may think. Sitting in that classroom at San Francisco State, I had a moment of Zen awakening. My life was utterly different before and after that moment.

In that moment of clarity, I knew in a flash that I could never be worthy to teach children unless my life changed at its root. I could not be the person I was meant to be or the person the world needed me to be if I didn't stop drinking. I needed to find within myself a rigorous honesty that would transform my present, my past, and my future. I later came to understand that I didn't need to discard or deny that wild and unbound time in my life, a time of travel and exploration, of seeking, disappointment, and doubt. All of it had been part of my path. As Dogen Zenji put it, "No increase, and no decrease, and no mistake."

Each of us is a unique human being, a collection of memories, experiences, knowledge, and relationships that exists nowhere else on earth or throughout space and time. At the same time, Zen practice has taught me that none of us exists for one moment without the help, the influence, the aid of myriad beings, of causes and conditions that we can never fully realize or apprehend. The trees lend their oxygen to me that I might live; the very ground supports my footsteps; I am made of stardust. I am supported by countless beings, most of whom I will never know.

In spite of my years of practice, I needed to find and work a program of recovery to maintain sobriety so that I could renew my Buddhist practice with greater clarity and integrity. I knew that without recovery, there could be no practice and no life. Recovery had to come first, and all else would follow. I found a sustaining group of sober people whose priority is to stay sober and to help others maintain a sober life. I learned that, to get and stay sober, I needed to admit that I needed help, to accept help from others, and once I had my feet firmly planted in sobriety, I needed to help others to maintain what I had fought so hard to achieve.

There may be some who have been able to maintain their sobriety solely through Buddhist practice. But my feeling is that millions of people, of many different cultures and religious persuasions, have been able to get sober without having to translate the words of recovery into the language of their own personal religion or system of belief. When I walk into the rooms of recovery, I am just another recovering alcoholic, like everyone else. Nothing special.

Well into my sobriety, I made amends to myself by returning to Alaska during the summertime. In my early twenties, I had ventured there on my own to see the wilderness and expand my world, a free woman on the loose. But I had stayed, instead, in the bars. I took a train to Bellingham, Washington, and boarded a ferry that would take me up the inland passage to Juneau. I slept in a sleeping bag on the deck and, by day, spotted seals, whales, and whirling seabirds as we made our way north. Staying with old friends in the Land of the Midnight Sun, I hiked and kayaked and enjoyed the beauty of that wild land. I also went to recovery meetings and told my story. To honor my previous dream to venture north and see the wilderness, I took the ferry up to Skagway, a small town that had been a setting-off point for those on their way to the Alaskan goldfields in the 1800s.

Whenever I go anywhere, I look for recovery meetings, so I went to Skagway's small library and asked the librarian if she could help me.

She said, patting my hand, "You know, dear, I've been sober for a while myself. We only have one meeting a week, and it was last night. I'll tell you what. Go around the corner, and you'll see a trailer there with a small house next to it. Knock on the door and ask for Mack."

I followed her directions and knocked on that door. A big man appeared in the doorway, wearing nothing but a pair of Levi's and holding a Diet Coke. Telling him that I was a friend in recovery, he invited me in and put on a black T-shirt. We sat at his kitchen table, sharing "war stories" and laughing as the afternoon slipped away.

Finally, I said to him, with tears in my eyes, "Mack, you and I couldn't be more different. You were a cop and a railroad man, and I'm a schoolteacher and a Buddhist. But we both did the same crazy things. And we both woke up."

"And that has made all the difference," he said.

Another transformation in my practice came when I asked Eijun Linda Cutts, senior dharma teacher and former abbess of Zen Center, to be my teacher. Her support, friendship, and love; her dedication to the dharma; and her unwavering faith in our practice have helped sustain me for many years.

Today, I try to live each day within the principles of recovery. I meditate regularly, and I meet with others so we can share this way of life with one another. I haven't had a drink since September 28, 1985. And there is no doubt in my mind that I could never have done this on my own, without the support of numberless others who also treasure recovery. You know who you are.

When I first came to Zen practice, I thought that I would have to "destroy a world," that I could simply put on a black robe and become someone else. But I have learned that practice blooms, as Dogen Zenji taught us, in this very mind and body. We don't have to shut the door on the past or become someone else, a better version of ourselves. In fact, we can share our past with others and give them hope that they too can step out of the darkness and into the light.

The Buddhist teacher Robert Thurman once said, "Practice isn't just about sitting on a cushion. It is about finding a kind of radical dharmic freedom. When faced with a choice, rather than responding instinctually, we pause and turn in the appropriate direction." A great gift of practice has been being able to work with other people in recovery and discover ways in which Buddhism can support a clean and sober life. Sobriety allows us to turn, again and again, in the appropriate direction.

As Nova was growing up, I taught school during the school year, and in the summer, I would return to Tassajara to join the sangha for zazen and service and to cook for the guests who came to visit the hot springs during the summer months. One night, with Nova asleep in the back seat, I drove over the mountains east of Big Sur on my way to the monastery, as Chris had so many years before. I stopped my car and got out to look at a night sky that was spangled with stars. I had struggled with the word *God*, which seems to happen to many of us in recovery, since we think of that word as the God of our childhood. I hadn't prayed in a long time, but on that mountain ridge, I said a prayer. Then I looked at the sky and said to myself, "If there is a God, I will see a shooting star *right now*." At just that moment, a shooting star blazed across the heavens. But I am an alcoholic. Never satisfied. So I said to myself, "If there *really* is a God, I'll see *another* shooting star." Nothing happened. But no matter how I might define God, with my limited understanding, the fact that one day I needed to drink and the next day I didn't is miracle enough for me.

In his book *Being Peace*, Thich Nhat Hanh says, "If we are peaceful, if we are happy, we can smile, and everyone in our family, our entire society, will benefit from our peace." This is an important reminder. We don't just claim peace and happiness as our birthright; rather, we rest in happiness and peace for the benefit of all beings. May we meet one another fully, face-to-face and heart-to-heart, as we walk this path of practice and recovery, finding our way together.

---

## Reflections and Practices

- Sit quietly in your zazen posture for a few minutes, coming back to your breath.
- Write your own Way Seeking Mind story. What was your family life like? Did you receive any religious or spiritual instruction? In your family, was there mental illness, alcoholism, or violence that affected you? What were your earliest experiences of using substances or engaging in dangerous or self-destructive behavior? What do you think you got out of that behavior? What were some

negative consequences of your acting out? Have you found a recovery program that works for you? What attracted you to Buddhist practice? What form does that practice take, and how has it informed your daily life?

- Many of us knew, long before we admitted it fully to ourselves, that we had a problem with addiction. Even while still using, we have had moments of clarity—looking in a mirror, seeing an expression on a loved one's face, waking up with a sinking feeling. Write about some of the moments of clarity you have had when acting out in your addiction.

- Developing a sitting practice and doing the work of recovery give us the ability to pause before acting. Think about a time when you responded impulsively to a situation and later regretted it. Think about a time when, instead of reacting impulsively, you were able to pause and turn in the appropriate direction.

# 2

---

# Shikantaza

The zazen I speak of is not learning meditation.
It is simply the dharma-gate of repose and bliss,
the practice-realization of totally culminated
    enlightenment.
It is the manifestation of ultimate reality . . .
            —Dogen Zenji, "Fukanzazengi," as chanted
                    at San Francisco Zen Center

THESE WORDS ARE OFFERED to us by Dogen Zenji (1200–1253), the Zen master and poet who founded the Soto school of Zen in Japan. In 1223, Dogen traveled to China where he studied for five years, eventually practicing with Rujing, known in Japan as Tendo Nyojo. When he heard Master Rujing say the words, "Cast off body and mind," Dogen was liberated, and this phrase echoed through the rest of his life and teachings. In "Genjokoan," Dogen says, "To study the Way is to study the Self. To study the Self is to forget the self. To forget the self is to be enlightened by all things of the universe. To be enlightened by all things of the universe is to cast off the body and mind of the self as well as those of others. Even the traces of enlightenment are wiped out, and life with traceless enlightenment goes on forever and ever."

Dogen returned to Japan to offer the practice of zazen, or *shikantaza*, and later founded Eihei-ji Monastery, which is the head temple of the Soto school to this day. Shikantaza is often referred to as "just sitting." It is a Japanese translation of a Chinese term for zazen that was used by Dogen's teacher, Rujing. *Shikantaza* has also been translated as "silent illumination" or "serene reflection." Suzuki Roshi said that shikantaza is just to be ourselves.

In 1959, Shunryu Suzuki Roshi (1904–1971), a Soto Zen priest, traveled from Japan to head the Japanese community at Sokoji Temple in San Francisco. Books by Alan Watts, D. T. Suzuki, and Paul Reps had introduced Zen to an American audience, and soon Western seekers began to make their way to Sokoji Temple to sit in the early morning with the enigmatic *roshi*, or Zen master, who could be by turns both fierce and playful. Suzuki Roshi was taken by the fresh curiosity and openness that he found in his Western practitioners, and he left Sokoji to form San Francisco Zen Center. Under his leadership, Zen Center later transformed a mountain retreat center in the Los Padres Wilderness into its monastery, Tassajara Zen Mountain Center. Green Gulch Farm is another branch of Zen Center, located in Marin. The residents there practice zazen in Green Dragon Temple, work on the organic farm, run the conference center, and care for the guests who come on retreat.

I visited Tassajara as a guest student during the summer in 1975, and when I came back to San Francisco, I was soon living at Zen Center, at the corner of Page and Laguna. This gracious brick building was designed by Julia Morgan as a residence for young Jewish women in the 1920s. After several months, I went to Tassajara for monastic training. During my years there, we hosted families for a year, and I was asked to teach the children in a one-room schoolhouse at the monastery. Later, this year of teaching inspired me to earn a teaching credential. I taught children for thirty-five years, first at Alvarado Elementary in San Francisco and then, until my retirement in 2020, at The San Francisco School.

Suzuki Roshi asked his students to "shine one corner of the world," and my third-grade classroom was the corner of the world that I endeavored to shine.

One day, during silent sustained reading, one of my students walked in front of my desk and did a little dance. I whispered to him, "Nathan, what were you thinking about just then?" and he answered, excited, "Laura, do you ever forget you are alive and suddenly you remember!"

Yes, Nathan, I do.

In zazen, leave your front door and your back door open. Let thoughts come and go. Just don't serve them tea.

—Suzuki Roshi

## Sitting Practice: The Heart of Zen

The heart of Zen practice is zazen, the simple practice of sitting still, breathing in and out, and experiencing the expansive nature of reality. In a Zen community, members gather in the temple zendo in the morning and evening to sit zazen with one another.

We enter and find our seat, whether on a cushion or a chair. We bow toward our sitting place to honor all those who have gone before us and to recognize and honor the practice of sitting and our own awakened nature. Then we turn in a clockwise direction and bow toward the assembly. We settle ourselves, sitting cross-legged on the zafu or upright in the chair, facing the wall, and listen for the bell that begins the meditation session.

Whether sitting in a chair or cross-legged on a zafu, we sit with a straight spine and strength in the lower back, with the pelvis tipped slightly forward. The shoulders are rolled back, the eyes slightly open, with a diffuse awareness. Hands rest in the lap, palms facing up. We use the Cosmic Mudra, with the back of the left hand resting on the right palm and the thumb tips lightly touching. It helps to imagine that a string is lifting from the crown of the head and the chin is tucked in a bit. The tongue rests on the back of the front teeth. The ears are in line with the shoulders, and the nose is in line with the navel. We inhale and exhale deeply and quietly, and sway to the left and right, or grasping our knees one after the other with the opposite hand, gently twist the spine. We take a few deep breaths and then allow the breath to assume its natural rhythm, breathing silently through the nose, not trying to control it in any way, just observing it. It is helpful to notice when the inbreath turns around and becomes an outbreath, and when the outbreath turns around and becomes an inbreath. We can enjoy the sensation in the chest and belly as the breath comes and goes.

We can focus on the breath by breathing in and then out through the nose, counting mentally "one." We breathe in, then out, counting "two," and so on, up to ten, and then we begin again. Should the mind wander—and it will—we gently come back to the breath. We sit with no idea of achieving anything, just sitting quietly with the breath. As thoughts, plans, regrets, and memories arise, we note them without suppressing them and gently let them recede into the background. In the words of Kosho Uchiyama Roshi, "Zazen is the best posture for truly aiming at reality as it is. Aiming at this posture of body and life, as it is, is also referred to as shikantaza—just sitting."

When the bell rings to signal the end of zazen, we bow in a particular way, called *gassho* in Japanese: we press the flattened palms together, fingers aligned, in front of the nose, elbows lifted slightly, and bend a little at the waist. While it is helpful to sit and practice with others, we can also sit on our own, in our own homes. Find a quiet spot in your home where you can sit regularly, and make sure that your family or housemates understand that this is time you are setting aside for yourself when you don't want to be interrupted. Having a meditation bell near your sitting place will be a helpful call to zazen. Let your mind rest on the sound of the bell.

After zazen, in a temple setting, the sangha gathers to bow and chant together. Each side of the room faces the other. The *kokyo* is the leader of the chanting, and other practitioners hit the drums and ring the bells. Each day is a little different. We might chant the Heart Sutra, the Diamond Sutra, the names of the Buddhas and Ancestors, the Loving-Kindness (or Metta) Sutra, the Homage to the Perfection of Wisdom. In chanting, we find one note and chant on that note, blending our voices together. If you are sitting at home, you will find some sutras for chanting in the back of the book.

As a focal point for your sitting, you may want to create a home altar. You can designate a shelf or table for this purpose. Cover it with a pretty cloth, add a candle and a vase of flowers. If you have a figure of the Buddha, Guan Yin, or another inspiring figure, you can place it in the center of your altar. This can also be a focal point for your family or friends, where you can celebrate the seasons, place leaves or shells you find in nature, and have photographs or mementos of loved ones who have died. I chant the Metta Sutta every morning at my home altar as part of my sitting practice, to help me set my intention for the day and to open my heart to the world.

At Zen Center, we sit for forty-minute periods, separated by ten minutes of walking meditation, or *kinhin*. If you are just starting this practice at home, you can begin with shorter periods of sitting, say ten or fifteen minutes, building up to longer sessions as you go. Most people find that early morning, before the demands of the day arise, is the best time to sit. At the end of each chapter of this book, I suggest you sit for a few minutes before engaging in the reflections and practices.

In the book *Not Always So*, Suzuki Roshi says, "I feel sorry that I cannot help you very much. But the way to study true Zen is not verbal. Just open yourself and give up everything. Whatever happens, whether you think it is good or bad, study closely and see what you find out. This the fundamental attitude. . . . Without losing yourself by sticking to a particular rule or understanding, keep finding yourself, moment after moment. This is the only thing for you to do."

---

## Reflections and Practices

- Using these instructions as a guide, begin to establish a sitting practice, if you haven't done so already. Begin at home with short sittings of five to ten minutes. You can begin to sit longer as you become more comfortable with the practice of zazen. Sitting first thing in the morning is a helpful way to begin each day with a kind of freshness, and sitting at the end of your day can be conducive to restful sleep.

- Another way to begin to establish your practice is to stop during your day and take three deep breaths. You will be surprised at the transformation that is possible as you bring these simple moments to your life.

# 3

## The Buddha's Story
## Is Our Story

The thought manifests as the word;
the word manifests as the deed;
the deed develops into habit;
and habit hardens into character.
So watch the thought and its ways with care,
And let it spring from love
Born out of concern for all beings.

—The Buddha in the *Dhammapada*

WHEN THE BUDDHA was asked, "Who are you? What are you?" he gave this simple answer: "I am awake."

In fact, the word *buddha* means just that—"one who has awakened." The Buddha spent his life offering his teachings to whoever wanted them, sharing wisdom that would help others awaken too. He said, "I teach about suffering and about an end to suffering."

Siddhartha Gautama was born around 563 B.C.E. in what is known today as Nepal. His father was a kind of feudal lord, and the boy grew up with every advantage one could imagine—great wealth, luxurious surroundings, and doting parents. In Buddhist texts, he is described as exceedingly handsome and graceful. His parents protected him from any experience that would reveal the suffering of the world. He was sheltered under white umbrellas and dressed in silk, and when he went beyond the palace gates, a servant ran ahead of his carriage to clear away anyone who was sick, old, or dying. At sixteen, he was married to his wife, Yasodhara, and they had a son, Rahula.

Despite his sheltered existence, when he was old enough to see for himself, Siddhartha was confronted with the truth of impermanence. Venturing on his own beyond the palace walls, he encountered sickness, old age, and death. He wondered why there was suffering and if there was any way to heal the suffering of the world. When he saw a luminescent monk with a begging bowl, he realized that there was an alternative to his pampered life. He left home, leaving his wife and child behind, to seek the world from which he had been protected.

Taking up the life of an ascetic, Siddhartha denied himself every pleasure and instead dressed in rags, ate little, traveled with other seekers, and sought out Hindu teachers who might help him. But as his body starved and he grew weaker, he realized that he could not penetrate the truth of existence without this very mind and body. It is said that at this moment of realization, a young girl came over the fields with a bowl of rice porridge.

"This is for you," she said simply.

This was the beginning of Siddhartha's embrace of the Middle Way, a way of life that was neither self-indulgent nor cruelly punishing; rather, one lived simply and with common sense.

Legend has it that Siddhartha traveled to Gaya, in Northeast India, and found his way to the foot of a peepul tree, a tree that is known today as the bodhi tree in honor of the Buddha's awakening. Vowing that he would not move until he had attained enlightenment, he sat down. Soon the frightening demonic figure of Mara appeared, bringing forth every kind of distraction, from dancing girls and tantalizing food to hurricanes and showers of flaming rocks. But Siddhartha sat still. Arrows rained down on him from armies in the sky, but as he looked up, they were transformed by his gaze into drifting flowers. Finally, when Mara challenged his very right to remain, unmoving, under the tree and to awaken, Siddhartha touched the ground and raised a hand toward the sky and the earth trembled, witnessing his deep intention. Mara vanished.

As he remained still, sitting through the night under the bodhi tree, his meditation deepened, and he perceived his profound interconnection with all life, with all beings. When he looked up and saw the morning star, the last shreds of his ignorance vanished, and he was at peace, at one with all things. He was awake.

When he stood up, he wanted to teach what he had learned to others. He found his companions, who saw that he glowed with a new wisdom, and his first teaching was the Four Noble Truths. In life there is great suffering, and the Buddha found that the cause of our self-created suffering is desire or craving, in Sanskrit, *tanha* (literally "thirst"). We are restless and unsatisfied, thirsting after some blissful moment in the future when we might finally be at peace. He taught that the way toward peace is in living in harmony with our inmost selves and with others, what the Buddha called the Noble Eightfold Path, a way to go forward with integrity, gratitude, and generosity, practicing these principles in all our affairs.

The Buddha's story is our story. When the Buddha leaves home to find the truth, we can recall the old ideas and family patterns that we had to leave behind as we set off on our own life's journey. When the Buddha touches the ground and raises a hand to the heavens, he is asserting not only his own right to awakening but confirming the potential for awakening that lives within each of us.

Though we may not have grown up in a palace in North India, if we want to wake up, we have to confront the truth of impermanence. Many of us have had a profound experience of loss and suffering that leads us to the source of the Buddha's teachings. We also must examine the stories that our family and our culture have told us and find our own path. This often involves the discomfort of displeasing the very people we spent our whole childhood trying to please. In this challenging world that demands so much of us, we may turn toward addictive behaviors to soothe ourselves and decrease our anxieties.

But addiction is the opposite of awakening. At first, it may seem to give us a new kind of freedom and abandon, but we can spend the rest of our lives chasing after that first innocent rush and never really finding it again, dealing instead with the consequences of actions taken under the influence—friends and families betrayed, our dreams unrealized. We may find ourselves in a seemingly unending loop of shame and guilt that leads us back to the illusion of relief that is offered by addictive behaviors. The figure of Mara in the Buddha's story seems like an external enemy that comes to taunt and tempt him. But we can see Mara as a kind of archetype, or symbol, of our own distracted nature. No one has to lure us away from our peace, stability, and concentration—we can do that ourselves. In our addiction, we cheat ourselves over and over again, stifling the voice inside that could awaken us to our inherent inner wisdom.

Transforming addiction into recovery requires the same sense of purpose, the same deep intention, the same piercing insight, that drove the Buddha to the foot of the bodhi tree. If we want to be released from this endless loop, we need to find within us the courage to sit down, as the Buddha did, and face the darkness. This includes recognizing the nature of addiction and the harm we have caused to ourselves and others because of it.

Many people identify so deeply with their addiction that they aren't sure who they would be without it. "Where will I find friends? What will I do for fun? How will I ease my fears and anxieties? How will I loosen up, and how will I be able to sleep at night?" But on the other side of this thick wall of denial is a world of light, of true friendship, of freedom, and of joy. If we can fully concede to our inmost self that we need help, if we can accept that help, and if we can then offer help to others, we can find a new kind of freedom and a life that we never imagined.

It's mysterious that someone can go through this painful revolving door of addiction, trying again and again to stop and not being able to, until one day they "hit bottom." They finally come to the end and awaken to the realization that if they don't stop and take another path, their life will continue to devolve into a kind of personal hell. Ironically, just on the other side of the darkest moment of their life, there is another reality waiting for them.

The first glimpse of recovery is awakening to the cause of our suffering and to the healing that is waiting for us. There is another way to live. Just as the Buddha taught.

## Reflections and Practices

- Sit quietly in your zazen posture for a few minutes, coming back to your breath.

- Before we come to practice and recovery, we inevitably have had many experiences of loss and grief. What we thought we could count on evaporates before us. Someone we loved dies or leaves us. An opportunity we longed for doesn't come through. Reflect on your experiences of impermanence and how they affected you. Write them down.

- Sometimes our failures end up leading to our true path. Write about something you dearly wished for that didn't come to pass but that led to a blessing you didn't anticipate. Perhaps a cherished relationship came to an end. You didn't get the job opportunity you were hoping for. You felt that you had failed at something, yet it led you toward a greater truth. Write about these experiences or share them with a trusted friend.

# 4

## Living from the Inside Out

Take the backward step that turns the light and shines it inward.

—Dogen Zenji, "Fukanzazengi"

PRACTICING BUDDHISM and recovery, we learn to live from the inside out. We learn to cultivate an inner integrity that guides us rather than being blown around by our impulses like branches torn apart in a cyclone. We have a sense of coming home. Even if we have been abandoned by others in the past, we learn that we don't have to abandon ourselves. Once we have learned to recognize and yet not to act on our addictive impulses, we learn how to cope with strong feelings when they arise rather than denying them, pushing them away, or self-medicating.

I think I felt that, with Buddhist practice, I could glide over difficult feelings and experiences with a serene smile on my face. That I could put on a black robe and chant in Japanese and be someone else. I thought it might be easier to become someone else than it was to be myself. But that didn't work for me. I needed to feel things deeply and fully so that I could live deeply and fully. What I learned in recovery is that I don't have to act on my feelings to be authentically myself. Paradoxically, that means that I can confront feelings honestly, knowing that they won't destroy me or the people around me, because I can decide when it is appropriate to act on them.

The Buddha taught the great truth of impermanence, this tender sadness that comes with being alive. Friends die, children grow up, we face rejection and loss, those whom we love let us down, we feel mad or sad or incomplete. If we can deeply accept these feelings and walk through them to the other side, we build strength within ourselves that we can share with others. We stay with that sadness rather than being ashamed of it or trying to make it go away. We make friends with what we might have previously rejected in ourselves and others, going wide-eyed into those dark places, knowing that we will survive. And we get that, whatever is happening, this too shall pass. I learned that nothing that could happen to me would be improved with the addition of alcohol. When I got sober, I heard people say, "You don't have to drink if you don't want to." But I was more relieved to hear, "You don't have to drink even if you *do* want to."

"All that you love will be carried away." I wish I could say that I read that in the sutras, but this phrase appears as graffiti in a phone booth in a Stephen King story. If we hold this truth at the center of our lives, we will be more likely to seize the present moment and love the ones we love more fiercely, knowing that all of this is temporary. We will be more likely to honor our commitments, find our own path, express our creativity, and help those we can help.

Vine Deloria Jr., the Native American author, theologian, and activist, is credited with saying, "Religion is for those who are afraid of going to hell. Spirituality is for those who have already been there." If you have a history of struggling with substances, self-destructive behavior, or the addictions of those you love, you have been to hell. This gives you a unique ability to connect with others who are in hell and offer a hand in the darkness. It is only by being true to what we see in the dark that we can emerge into the light, whole again and able to reach out to others. Much of this strength comes from finding and practicing with others who want what we want.

A story about heaven and hell, "the allegory of the long spoons," appears in many religions and cultures. In hell, the people sit at tables piled high with delicious, fragrant food. But because each of them has a spoon that is longer than their arm, they can't get the food close enough to their mouths to eat it, and so they starve. In heaven, people sit at tables piled high with delicious, fragrant food. Each of them has a spoon that is longer than their arm, and they are happily using their spoons to reach across the table and feed one another. While recovery is an "inside job," we can't underestimate the importance of the nourishment we receive from others in our program. In recovery, we live with this paradox. We live life with greater integrity, from the inside out. But we also learn how to open ourselves to the help of others.

My first Buddhist teacher stopped me outside the meditation hall one morning and told me, "You have everything you need. Just stop looking for answers outside yourself." This was an invitation to start living from the inside out. In that moment, the true gift of Buddhism began to manifest for me because I came to understand that this ancient path doesn't ask me to withdraw my common sense, to subscribe to a particular set of beliefs, or to follow a teacher mindlessly.

In Soto Zen, the emphasis is on just sitting. Just sitting down in the middle of our lives. Each time we sit down, we honor and affirm our own gift of awakening, our own inherent ability to wake up. We honor those who went before us, both in practice and in recovery, because their persistence and dedication come down to us as a gift. We sit with our whole selves, with this very mind and body, not with some ideal self that we might achieve some day. Dogen said, "This very mind is Buddha," not some other, better mind that awaits us.

When I stepped into the zendo the first time, I did so with the hope that Buddhism would fix me, make me better, help me live a better life. I would dive into the ancient stream of Buddhist practice, leaving my broken self behind. This is "outside-in" thinking, using practice in a mechanical "fix-it" kind of way.

That was how I had used alcohol—bringing something outside myself into my body to make me feel better. The word *intoxicate* means "to bring poison in." When I used Buddhism in this same way, as a kind of antidote to the way I actually felt and who I actually was, trying to fix myself and deny the rejected parts of myself, my practice was hollow and—though well-intentioned—lifeless.

In Buddhism and our work in recovery, we can start living dynamically, from the inside out. In "Fukanzazengi," Dogen says, "Take the backward step that turns the light and shines it inward." This is counter to everything our culture tells us. We are told that happiness and success lie in getting all the good stuff that is out there. It doesn't matter how you get it; you can lie, cheat, and steal. The most important thing is not to be a "loser." When we step onto the path of practice and recovery, we can stop looking outside ourselves for satisfaction; we can mine for riches at the vivid center of our own lives.

Buddhism teaches us that to be alive is to lose. "All that you love will be carried away." The things we cling to and identify with and think will last don't. Yet we can find peace and serenity amid that loss. The only place we can rest is in this very moment, living deeply and richly and fully right now, meeting each person and event with an open heart. This is where we have a chance to meet joy, to come home to our breath and our true nature. And we can do this with others rather than in a stagnant pool of self.

Whenever I get the blues and sit down and watch that happening, I am often engaging in outside-in thinking. Judging myself by some outside standard. Regretting the past. Fearing the future. This is when the corrosive habits of resentment and self-pity take root. When I begin to expect things of others that they probably don't even know about. When I start to expect things of myself that I haven't yet taken the time to put in place. Forgiving myself, forgiving others, and recognizing that we are all just doing the best we can help me return to living from the inside out.

I couldn't fully come to Buddhism until I got sober and did the work—the self-examination and the actions to be taken—that recovery required.

First, I had to do that from the inside out. Not because I wanted to please people I loved. Not to be a better mother. Not to become a better person. I had to admit deeply this fundamental truth: that I am an alcoholic and can never drink like other people, something I proved to myself time and again. I have met other Buddhists who reject the word *alcoholic* or are uncomfortable with it, maybe because they don't want to label themselves.

Maybe because they feel that, to practice Buddhism, they need to drop their personal story.

For me, all my freedom and joy spring from being able to honestly admit this undeniable fact. I had to be willing to become who I actually am. I knew I couldn't do that and continue to drink. I needed to remember my story and tell it to others, so I would never again forget where I came from. And to give others the chance to identify with my story so they would know that recovery is within reach.

Second, I had to be willing to ask for help. At the very end of my drinking, something called out from the depths of my being, "Please, please help me." I didn't know then that I was on the threshold of awakening to a power within myself that I hadn't been able to access.

Third, I had to be willing to accept help. This required the annihilation of any form of intellectual pride. I had to put aside everything I thought I knew about myself and be willing to open myself to, and learn from, other people who had discovered how to stay sober. In many cases, these were people who seemed to be very different from me. Yet we shared this disease and the potential to overcome it.

Fourth, I had to be willing to offer others the same help that had been so freely given to me. I had to reach out into the darkness and help pull other suffering people into the lifeboat of recovery.

In the actions I took in recovery, I began to find a deep inner resource within me, because of this path of rigorous honesty, self-reflection, and action that had not been available to me, despite years of meditation and Buddhist study.

Finally, I had to not be afraid of the word *God*, which often comes up in recovery programs. I had to cultivate the humility to accept things that my intellectual pride might have rejected. For someone who had turned her will and her life over to the care of alcohol, it seemed a little hypocritical to think that I couldn't get sober if I had to be in a room where people say that word. The word *God* simply points to a mystery that, to stay sober, I don't need to define or resist. In Zen we say, "A finger pointing at the moon is not the moon." The word *God* is a finger pointing at something we can never fully comprehend with our limited human understanding.

The collective intention to stay sober that I find in the rooms of recovery gives me the strength to take refuge in Buddha, Dharma, and Sangha, the Three Jewels of Buddhism. Taking refuge in Buddha is having faith in my own inherent awakeness. Taking refuge in Dharma is letting go and accepting what Suzuki Roshi called "things as it is." Taking refuge in Sangha is finding solace in connection and community. Taking refuge in the Three Jewels is a power greater than myself, and that is all I need to know.

Buddhism is an invitation to return to our common sense, to see things as they are, without lying to ourselves about what is or fantasizing about what might be. To fully enter the present moment, eyes wide open, and respond appropriately to what life asks of us. I would say that recovery asks nothing less.

When I was seven, my father and brother and I traveled by car across the United States from New York to California. We stopped at a county fair in the Midwest and roamed around, drinking milk right from a cow and going on rides. One was a "teacup" ride. My brother Peter and I climbed into a giant teacup, and the man who ran the ride turned it on; the teacups began to spin around. My dad was a friendly guy, and he went over to shoot the breeze with the man running the ride. Dad had his back to us, so he didn't see me thrashing around in the teacup, my hair flying around, as I howled in terror. My brother tried to show me how to brace myself by holding on to the safety bar, but I didn't get it.

Finally, thankfully, the ride stopped, and I wiped the tears from my face and tried to smooth my tangled hair. For me, that experience later became a metaphor for the way I had gone through life at the mercy of my strong emotions and random experiences, never realizing that I could protect myself by developing a strong inner guide that would encourage me to live from the inside out. That I could "brace myself" with the safety bar offered to me by the sober beings who had gone before me and by the ancient Zen practice that allows me to be fully myself.

---

## Reflections and Practice

- Sit quietly in your zazen posture for a few minutes, coming back to your breath.

Write about these reflections or invite a friend to explore them with you:

- At what times in your life have you felt abandoned?
- At what times have you abandoned yourself?
- When did you have to find your own way, going against what others thought you should do? What was the outcome?

# 5

# Kintsugi: The Places We Are Broken

The wound is where the light enters you.
—Rumi

THE ZEN TEA MASTER Sen no Rikyu was traveling through southern Japan and was invited to dinner by a man who wanted to impress him with an elaborate antique jar. Rikyu, though, didn't seem to notice the jar, but spoke poetically about a branch swaying in the breeze outside. He said his goodbyes and went on his way. Frustrated, the host held up the jar and hurled it to the floor, where it broke into many jagged shards.

The host turned to go to bed as his startled guests looked at one another. Gathering up the fragments, they joined them together using lacquer infused with gold, a technique that became known as *kintsugi*. When Rikyu returned on another visit and saw the repaired jar with the veins of gold highlighting the broken places he exclaimed, "*Now* it is magnificent!"

One of my earliest impressions of Zen Buddhism was an article I saw in a magazine about the practice of kintsugi. The syllable *kin* means "golden," and *tsugi* means "joinery, to join with gold." When repairing a broken teacup, rather than disguising or hiding the broken places, they are highlighted, contributing to a new kind of beauty. The practice of kintsugi belongs to the Japanese ideal of *wabi-sabi*, the appreciation of objects that are simple and unpretentious, with a rustic, aged quality. Wabi-sabi recognizes the beauty of things that are incomplete, imperfect, well-worn, and venerable.

The great Sufi poet Rumi said, "The wound is where the light enters you." All of us are slightly cracked. All of us have places in us that are broken, incomplete, wounded, imperfect. Sometimes we forget that the places in us that are broken are the very places where we can connect with other people.

If we have suffered a terrible grief, we are uniquely qualified to reach out and help others who are grieving. If we have experienced a great loss (and we all have), we can comfort those who have lost. If we have been through a life-changing trauma, we can help those who are going through a dark and difficult time. If we have overcome addiction, we can help someone else who is struggling. When we turn around, face our own lives, and move toward healing, those places in us that are broken glow with a kind of golden thread.

We don't sit zazen to try to improve ourselves, to perfect ourselves, to become a different or better version of ourselves. Rather, we sit to be exactly who we are. Though we don't sit with any idea of gain, we do come to know ourselves in an intimate way, all our flaws and cracks—and the places in us that are seamed with gold.

Part of this knowing ourselves, part of healing the broken places, is waking up to the way we treat other people. Without being aware of it, we may be responding to others in a habitual way that pushes them away from us rather than allowing them to come closer. Many of us developed coping skills in childhood that protected us. Now, we can begin to loosen these protective barriers as we get more comfortable in our own skin.

I learned a Mexican proverb from my friend Chay when I was studying Spanish in Oaxaca:

> Each person has four parts:
> The part that everyone knows,
> The part that only that person knows,
> The part that everyone but that person knows,
> And the part that nobody knows.

Working with others can give us a glimpse of the part of us that everyone is aware of—except us. Anyone can be peaceful and serene on a mountaintop, but it is in relationship with others that we can truly see ourselves. Sometimes others see special qualities in us that we are blind to. And sometimes they can help us see the places where we are broken, the ways in which we push others away, returning to the painful isolation we've created when what we long for is intimacy.

Addiction is a disease of isolation, and sometimes we sabotage relationships, ensuring that isolation. We may be broken in ways that make it difficult to create wholesome relationships with others. In our families of origin, we may not have had the best role models for what a mature relationship can look like. We grew up thinking that whatever we witnessed at home was "normal," having nothing else to compare it to. Conflict in our family of origin might have been so dangerous and threatening that we now avoid conflict at any cost. We may have inherited unskillful ways of relating to others and feel justified in that behavior because we feel we haven't been treated so well ourselves. If we want to move toward a way of relating that encourages peace, harmony, and reconciliation, it is important to look closely at and shift these habitual ways of being.

How can we mend our brokenness? How can we be agents of peace in our own lives?

The work of John Gottman, PhD, has been embraced by the Greater Good Science Center at the University of California, Berkeley. Dr. Gottman has done research on what constitutes a healthy marriage. This thinking is aimed at healthy love relationships, but the principles can be applied to any relationship, those you have with your friends, with your children, with your family, or at work. Dr. Gottman refers to four unhelpful responses as "The Four Horsemen" as in The Four Horsemen of the Apocalypse in the Bible. These responses, which are all too human, tend to destroy intimacy rather than creating it. They are:

Criticism
Contempt
Defensiveness
Stonewalling

# 1. Criticism

It's probably impossible to have a healthy relationship unless we can find a way to bring up and deal with conflict. For each person to be heard and get their needs met, there should be the trust and freedom to air complaints and concerns. Where this becomes a problem is when there is a tendency to criticize our friend/partner/family member in a broad way, making negative judgments or proclamations about their character or personality rather than focusing on a particular issue. You know you might be doing this if you find yourself using words like *always* or *never*. If you say, "You never think about anyone but yourself," you are probably not telling the whole truth. At the same time, you are putting the other person in the position of defending their very being. Since they know it isn't true that they never think of anyone but themselves, it makes it harder for them to take seriously what might be a reasonable complaint.

When bringing a problem to light, it's probably best to focus on your own feelings and to share the effect your friend's/partner's/coworker's actions have on you. For example, "I feel discouraged when I have dinner waiting, and you don't let me know that you will be late," rather than, "You are so selfish and inconsiderate."

When we approach conflict or difficulty with love and genuine curiosity about the other person's feelings, we have a very different outcome. Rather than speaking in the heat of the moment, it makes sense to set up a time to talk after you have both cooled off and had time to think. Inviting the other person to share their feelings with us, to demonstrate that we are really listening and hearing, we engage in active listening. Listening deeply to the other person requires staying with them in the present moment.

Too often we can find ourselves thinking about what we want to say next rather than really hearing the other person. The process of active listening can sound a little forced or self-conscious at first, until you get used to it:

1. Paraphrase what the person tells you, putting it in your own words, without embellishment, to make sure you are getting what that person is saying.
2. Ask appropriate questions.
3. Express empathy in a natural way.
4. Use engaged body language rather than leaning back with your arms crossed.
5. Avoid judgment and giving advice.
6. Take turns. Once you feel you've really listened to and heard the other person's concerns, ask if you can share your point of view with them.

To build a healthy, supportive relationship, Dr. Gottman recommends making the effort to have five positive interactions for every negative or critical interaction.

## 2. Contempt

Contempt for our partner/friend/child/coworker is communicated in our tone of voice and body language. Contempt can take the form of ridicule, sarcasm, eye-rolling, name-calling, or a harsh and condemning tone of voice. In a long-term relationship/friendship/work relationship, we cultivate contempt when we focus on the negative, on the qualities we don't like in the other person. We can hang on to small resentments and allow them to fester, then lash out at inappropriate times and in inappropriate ways.

If this is your tendency, remind yourself often about what you appreciate about the other person rather than obsessing on the negative.

- What are you grateful for in your relationship?
- How has the other person been there for you in times of need?
- How did you become close in the first place?
- What qualities do you value in this person?

## 3. Defensiveness

When we are criticized, even in a kind and skillful way, it is easy to go into a defensive stance rather than taking responsibility for our own part in a conflict. We can lash out to defend ourselves or start enumerating the wrongs of the other person, listing grievances from the past. When we respond in this all-too-understandable way, the other person doesn't feel heard, understood, or valued. It takes humility to drop the armor we've developed over many years and instead listen with an open mind, learning how we might have harmed another and responding with openness. This can be as simple as realizing that we don't always have to be "right."

- This is another place for active listening.
- Take the time to listen to and reflect the other person's concerns.

- Take responsibility when appropriate.
- Remember that we lose nothing by making a sincere apology, which can go a long way to healing a conflict.

## 4. Stonewalling

We can respond to a conflict with another person by withdrawing—by stonewalling, shutting down, physically and emotionally distancing ourselves from the other person without explanation, giving them the "silent treatment," leaving without saying where we're going or when we will be back. All these passive-aggressive behaviors make the other person feel abandoned and rejected.

We may have witnessed such behavior among adults when we were children. It may even have been directed at us by a frustrated parent. The adults in our lives might have felt that this kind of behavior was preferable to erupting in anger or even violence, but it didn't address the conflict in a helpful way. If this is your tendency, you can try some alternatives:

- You can say that you are interested in hearing the other person's point of view and are willing to talk but that you need some time.
- If you feel you can't engage in a positive way right now, say when you might feel ready. Offer to return to the conversation later.
- Take a few deep breaths and collect your thoughts; go for a walk outdoors; smell a rose; drink a cool glass of water; look up at the vast sky; lean against a tree.

- In this way, you communicate that you are taking care of yourself and being thoughtful rather than rejecting the other person by turning away from them.

If we become aware of the ways we express contempt, criticize harshly, act defensive, or withdraw from others, we will see some of the subtle ways we inflict hurt on those we love, often without meaning to, just by responding in unskillful ways.

Ernest Hemingway pointed out that the world breaks all of us and that many of us are stronger at the broken places. Let us treasure the cracked and mended teacups that we all are and let us shine with the golden threads of awakening.

---

## Reflections and Practices

- Sit quietly in your zazen posture for a few minutes, coming back to your breath.

Write your responses to these questions or share them with a trusted friend:

- Do you still hear the critical, contemptuous, sarcastic voice of a parent or partner in your own head?
- Do you sometimes hear yourself mirroring this negative voice with others?
- What were the relationship models you grew up with?
- How was anger expressed in your household?

- Do you recognize these four unskillful ways of dealing with conflict from your own family of origin? Is one of the ways a particular tendency of yours?
- How would you like to transform your intimate relationships so they are more harmonious and nurturing for yourself and others?

# 6

# Straw into Gold

We run and run from who we are, only to discover, of course,
that that is precisely what we can never put behind us.

—Pico Iyer

WHEN WE SIT ZAZEN, we sit still in the middle of a crazy world.
Not leaning to the left or the right. Not leaning forward or back.
Just sitting. We watch what arises, not running away, return-
ing again and again to the breath. When we sit, we voluntarily
embrace a certain limitation. Sitting still with a straight spine.
Sitting in a particular way. Choosing, for a time, not to do what
we usually do. Sitting alone or with others. Within this limita-
tion, we can taste a very real freedom.

By finally choosing another limitation, the decision not to drink
or use drugs, my true freedom as a human being began. In recov-
ery, we learn to pause and reflect before we mindlessly repeat the
pattern of habitual self-destructive behavior. We have the freedom
to turn in a wholesome direction, to call a friend in recovery, to go

to a meeting, to reach out to a power greater than ourselves. We vow to practice this pause, this turn, again and again, no matter what we are confronted with in life. This is the alchemy of recovery.

As a practicing alcoholic, I was in the thrall of my instincts, like a character in a fairy tale who is under a curse or a magic spell. I never fully experienced freedom from this curse until I got sober because, until I entered the rooms and began to work with others toward recovery, I had only illusory periods of relative freedom. Always, after a month, or a year, or five years, I picked up the next drink.

Stories from our Western tradition can be windows into the recovery process. In "Rumpelstiltskin," the familiar Grimm's fairy tale, a miller is chatting with the king. Wanting to impress his ruler, the miller mentions that his daughter can spin straw into gold. The very next day, the king installs her in a dim room with a spinning wheel and a pile of straw.

"Now spin!" he tells her. "Or tomorrow, you will die!"

The poor girl begins to cry piteously. She doesn't know how to spin straw into gold. Just then a funny little man appears.

"Good evening, miller's daughter," he says, tipping his hat.

"How did you get in here?" asks the miller's daughter. "This room is locked."

"No matter," says the little man. "Listen to me. If you give me your necklace, I will spin this pile of straw into a pile of gold."

Without a thought, she places the trinket in his hand. He sits down at the spinning wheel, and—whir, whir, whir—the pile of straw is transformed into a pile of glimmering gold.

This goes on for two more nights, the little man appearing and the miller's daughter offering him her bracelet and her ring in exchange for his magic.

Finally, the king tells her if she can spin one more roomful of straw into gold, she will become his queen. That night she rashly agrees to give the little man her firstborn child if he will spin the last pile of straw into gold. For who knows if she really will be queen? And if she does become queen, who knows if she will ever have a child?

The little man does his work, and the next day the king keeps his promise and marries the miller's daughter. A year later, the queen gives birth to a girl.

One evening, the queen is playing with her beautiful little girl when the little man appears to exact his reward. When the queen begins to cry, a tiny corner of his heart melts, and he tells her that if she can guess his name in three days, he will go away and never bother her again. Of course, he knows that she will never guess correctly!

The next night, when he returns, she gives him every name she can think of, and the following night as well. "No, no, no, that's not my name!" crows the little man.

So the queen sends a servant out to look far and wide, to collect the strangest names he can find. When the servant returns, he tells the queen that, as he made his way through a mountain pass, he saw a very peculiar sight. He saw a funny little man, dancing around a fire and singing:

Today my flour I make, tonight my bread I bake,
Tomorrow, tomorrow, tomorrow, the queen's little baby I take,
For lucky I go, as lucky I came, Rumpelstiltskin is my name!

When the little man appears that evening, the queen is waiting for him, sitting in the garden with her daughter on her lap.

"Well, miller's daughter, this is your last chance! Can you guess my name?"

The queen smiles. "Is it . . . Balthazar?"

"No!"

"Is it Thibault?"

"No!"

"Is it, could it be, are you . . . Rumpelstiltskin?"

With that, the little man bursts into a furious rage, sputtering and howling. He stomps his feet so hard that a hole in the earth opens beneath him and swallows him into the darkness, never to be seen again.

In this story, the miller makes an offhand comment to the king, trying to impress him. The daughter must then take up the burden of her father's unlived life, having been given a life-threatening challenge to do the impossible and spin straw into gold. (We won't even get into the fact that she must marry someone who threatens her with death.) We never even learn her real name—she is "the miller's daughter" and then "the queen"—and it is her father's offhand comment that condemns her to a small, dark room. We might say that the miller projects his unexpressed creativity, his own wish for fame and fortune, onto his unwitting daughter. Like some parents, he unconsciously tries to live his life through his child.

Many of us who grew up in abusive or alcoholic homes swore we would never repeat the patterns we grew up with, patterns shown to us by the adults in our lives. Sometimes the very pain of growing up around addiction, violence, or mental illness led us toward self-medication. It might have been our genetic destiny to turn toward addiction. It can be mystifying to find that, despite our best intentions, we are repeating the ancient, twisted karma of our family history.

The little man does this miraculous thing, spinning straw into gold. At first, our addiction seems to give us what we don't have—euphoria, self-confidence, expansiveness, courage. We bargain with addiction, giving away little parts of ourselves in exchange for the big yes of addiction. But in the end, one by one, addiction takes away from us all the things it seemed to promise us at first.

The miller's daughter offers the little man a necklace and a ring, but as time goes by, she forgets her enormous debt to him, the debt that must be paid. Finally, he returns to her and demands what she promised—the most precious thing she has, this beautiful child.

From the point of view of addiction, you might say that we are finally asked to give over the most precious things we have—our hope, our life force, our future. In the story, these things are symbolized by the newborn baby. Sadly, many who struggle with addiction have had to literally give up a child they were unable to care for.

We might have seen addiction as freedom and sobriety as a limitation. But each of us finally came to a fork in the road and had to choose between the limitation of addiction and the freedom of recovery. What does the miller's daughter have to do? She is presented with a rare opportunity, the opportunity to name this demon that wants to take everything from her. It is by naming this greedy little demon that she is finally free of him—and he is so angry and stomps so hard that he falls through a hole in the earth and, powerless, disappears. When I heard this story as a child, it was this white-hot anger that most frightened me. Could you really get so mad that you could stomp a hole in the earth and fall in, never to be seen again?

Our addiction begins to lose its power over us when we finally turn toward it and give it a name, when we concede to our inmost selves that what we thought was gold was really straw. We understand now that this elixir, so magical and life-affirming at first, wants to take away the most precious thing we have—life.

Saint Thomas quotes Jesus as saying, "If you bring forth that which is within you, that which you bring forth will save you. If you do not bring forth that which is within you, what you do not bring forth will destroy you." If we are under the spell of addiction, we are unable to fully call forth the precious potential that resides within us. We are trapped. Many addicts speak of the narrow little lives they find themselves in at the end of their time using, like the dark, confined room the miller's daughter finds herself in.

Our recovery, our practice begins when we turn and face the little man, the demon, the monster, the dragon, Mara, and give it a name, its true name: addiction. We find a world of freedom on the other side of a thick wall, but first we must name our demon.

Until I named this demon that controlled me, I had no true freedom. I was locked, powerless, in a little room, the dark little room that our addiction takes us to. Just by being willing to identify as an alcoholic, just by miraculously being willing to accept help, and just as miraculously by being able to offer help later, I began to walk the path of freedom.

Gandhi said, "God is Truth." In the work of recovery, confronting our illusions and admitting the truth is essential. Giving things the correct name is essential. I found that what I thought was righteous indignation was self-centered fear. That what I thought was freedom was selfishness. That when I harmed others, I also harmed myself. Writing these things down and sharing them with another human being was a tremendous relief. I could step out of the chaos of addiction with something precious to offer the world. A pinpoint of peace, of awakening.

Addiction is contagious in the sense that it seems to affect different members and generations of the same family. If we are in the thrall of addiction, we tend to gravitate toward the comfort of being with other addicts. But recovery is also contagious, passed from warm hand to warm hand. We encourage one another. We influence others in a positive way, often without even being aware of it. We walk the path of recovery together. We shine a light on one small corner of the world to reach out and help another suffering person. We taste the sweetness of our freedom and the universe that is open to us despite limitations.

This is spinning straw into gold.

---

## Reflections and Practices

- Sit quietly in your zazen posture for a few minutes, coming back to your breath.
- Write about what addictive behavior seemed to give you at the beginning.
- Write about what it has taken away from you.
- What is within you that you would you like to call forth? Have you been able to call forth something that was previously unavailable to you? Have you been able to express your freedom, wisdom, and creativity in new ways?
- What are you grateful for about practice and recovery?

# 7

## Eight Worldly Dharmas

Is that so?

—Hakuin Zenji

IN THE LOKAVIPATTI SUTTA, the Buddha teaches about the Eight Worldly Dharmas, sometimes called the Eight Worldly Winds. These are pairs of opposites that we tend to either cling to or push away: pleasure and pain, loss and gain, fame and disgrace, praise and blame. I can think of other seemingly opposing forces that exert themselves on our everyday lives—love and hate, ease and distress, hope and fear—but these eight can stand for the dance we do with the things we crave and the things we want to avoid.

The first of the Four Noble Truths is that in life there is suffering—anguish, discontent, dissatisfaction. Against the backdrop of the Eight Worldly Dharmas, we can see how our ordinary suffering takes shape. We cling to pleasure, gain, fame, praise; we disavow pain, loss, disgrace, blame. We walk a tightrope, trying to heap up praise and success, while we turn our backs on loss and pain.

We don't even notice that we are making up a lot of this stuff. Planning for a pleasure that may never materialize. Bracing ourselves against a disgrace that may never come our way. Sometimes our overreaction to these Eight Worldly Dharmas is based on experiences we've had in the past rather than anything that is happening right now. A remembered humiliation can warp our reaction to a benign event in our lives. The withholding of praise by a judgmental parent can make us crave it from those who don't owe it to us. We can find ourselves swimming around in a subjective reality that triggers our emotional responses, feeling blame where there is none, seeking pleasures that are fleeting at best.

There may be a temptation to turn away from these dharmas or to imagine that we can annihilate them, to regret them, to try to be aloof from them, to scold ourselves for getting seduced by them. "I should be further along in my practice by now. I've been sober for a long time, but I'm still getting pushed around by these strong feelings." Instead, we can start to see how the dharmas provide a rich vein of practice and recovery, a window into our own minds and emotions. There are many ways to practice in the swirl of these dichotomies.

One way is to accept that they are part of our everyday lives, that we tend to fall from side to side into these opposites. As we practice, as we observe the dance, we stop falling so far and can come back to a state of equanimity with a little more grace. We might even be able to laugh at ourselves a little bit, to take a deep breath and not take ourselves quite so seriously.

Another way is to watch what happens to our equanimity when we get off-balance. Our habits of mind/body are so deeply ingrained that, without practice, we can remain unconscious of them. With careful observation, we can see how we get jerked around by forces over which we have little control.

A third way is to notice how we create great dramas in our mind when we suffer a loss or enjoy a gain, when we experience pleasure or pain, when we feel we are respected in fame or in disgrace, when we see how we get puffed up with praise or deflated with blame. Often the drama comes when we aren't even actually experiencing these things but imagining that we will. We envision people praising us for something we may—or may not—accomplish in the future, or we imagine they are blaming us for some future or past omission or misdeed. We have conversations and disagreements in our minds with people who aren't even there.

The funny thing is, I don't think other people are thinking about us all that much.

It is probably a biological imperative that we foresee dangers so we can prepare for them. But if you are like me, you probably overdo it. When my daughter was little and we would enter a playground, I would look around and predict every danger that could possibly be lurking there. Luckily, Nova ignored me and just ran off to play.

We make ourselves suffer by imagining that we might lose something, that someone we love will leave us or be harmed in some way. When my brother, Peter, suffered an unforeseen tragedy, he said to me, "You spend your whole life worrying about things that never happen. Then something happens that you couldn't possibly have predicted. So why worry?"

We suffer when our expectations about life aren't in alignment with the way things actually are. Kosho Uchiyama Roshi, in his Zen classic *Opening the Hand of Thought*, says, "It's important to see that it's not life that causes suffering but our expectation that life should be the way we want. We can't live without expectation, but if we can handle the feelings caused by the difference between our expectations and reality, that's liberation. Zazen practice as taught by Dogen Zenji is taking a break from watching the screen of our stories and sitting down on the ground of the reality that exists before our imagination. When we're not taken in by our fictitious world, we can enjoy and learn from the stories we make."

Of course, one kind of antidote to our self-created suffering is just staying right here with the present moment, turning toward the events at hand. When we do that, we are better able to face and respond to what is going on right now, and we are also better prepared to respond appropriately to whatever might arise in the future.

I told this story to my third graders: "Imagine that you are in a car going down a steep hill. You are in the driver's seat, but the steering wheel doesn't seem to be working. You pump the brakes, but nothing happens. The road takes a sharp turn just ahead of you. What do you do?" The answer, of course, is . . . stop imagining!

Our sitting practice gives us the stability to notice when the mind is leaning toward or away from things. If we are craving the behavior or substance that has troubled us in the past, we know the craving will dissipate if we don't act on it. In our sitting practice and our recovery work, we manifest a kind of equanimity— neither grasping at what we want nor turning away in aversion from what we don't want. We sit upright in the middle of a suffering world. This posture is, itself, awakening,

I'd like to look a little more closely at praise and blame.

When I first came to Zen practice in 1975, I heard many intriguing and mystifying Zen stories. I remember wondering if they were holding the sutras upside down when they translated them, because they really didn't make much sense to me.

But as I continued to practice, now and then a story would flash into my mind and become useful to me. One of those stories is that of Hakuin Zenji, a wild man, a Zen priest, and a poet. I first became acquainted with Hakuin in the pages of *Zen Flesh, Zen Bones: A Collection of Zen and Pre-Zen Writings* by Paul Reps. Here is my version of Hakuin's story:

Hakuin Zenji lived in a mountain valley by the banks of a wide river. Before daybreak, he would meditate as the light of the moon slipped away and the light of the sun crept over the land. Each day, he took his alms bowl and meandered through sleepy villages nearby. In his own way, he was quite content, writing verses and singing songs that only he could hear.

One day, a distraught man and woman came to see him. The woman held in her arms a small baby.

"You call yourself a Zen priest?" growled the man. "Our daughter says that you are the father of her child! Disgraceful!"

"Is that so?" replied Hakuin. The man and woman placed the baby in his arms and, without another word, made their way back to their village.

Hakuin grew to love the child he had received and did his best to take care of him, weaving a basket for him to sleep in and sharing goat's milk and, later, scraps of food from his begging bowl with him.

After about a year, the man and woman returned, their heads bowed in shame.

"Hakuin Zenji, we are so sorry. Our daughter has admitted that it was not you who fathered her child—it was a young fisherman from our village. They have married, and we have come to take their child back to them. What a wonderful monk you are to have raised this child without complaint!"

Hakuin only smiled and said, "Is that so?"

He gently handed the boy back to his grandparents.

This story came vividly to mind for me at a difficult time during my teaching career when the parent of one of my students conceived a resentment toward me, writing a twelve-page letter to the school's board of directors that enumerated the imagined abuses I had heaped on her daughter. Luckily, I had been at the school for several years and taught many of the board members' children. They didn't believe that I would make a sick child stand outside in the rain or do any of the other things I was accused of. If anyone had done these things to my daughter, I wouldn't have written a letter. I would have gone to the police.

I found this unfortunate woman taking up space in my mind. I worried about my reputation and wondered if anyone had doubts about me. I went to my teacher, Eijun Linda Cutts, and told her about what I was going through. We talked about Hakuin Zenji and about how we can weather the praise and blame of others. She gave me a jewel when she said, "If you want to know what ego is, watch what happens when you are unjustly accused."

I was accustomed to the praise and support of the children, parents, administrators, and colleagues at my school. I felt recognized, accepted, and celebrated for who I was and for the way I was able to reach children. I remember when Elsie ran up to me on the playground, threw her arms around me, and said, "Laura, where have you been all my life?" I much preferred praise to blame, fame to disgrace.

My teacher asked me, "Maybe you can brush off the blame of others, but what about when someone is going on about how great you are? Can you also brush that aside?" With that, Linda made the gesture of flicking something off her shoulders, like water off a duck's back. "Can we say, 'Is that so?' even when we are showered with praise?"

At the end of his life, Suzuki Roshi said to one of his students, "Don't worry. I know who I am." In the midst of praise and blame, do I know who I am? Not the best teacher, not the worst teacher, but sincerely trying to live by Buddhist precepts and the principles of recovery. Trying to meet each child, mind to mind and heart to heart. In the midst of praise and blame, we can turn back toward our Bodhisattva Vow, "I vow to live and be lived for the benefit of all beings."

We tend to think of praise as a positive thing and blame as a negative thing. But if we are acting in such a way as to please others and win their praise, we may feel a bit cheap and hypocritical. There are also times when blame might be well placed; we need to listen carefully when constructive criticism is offered and see where we might be wrong. Sitting upright in the midst of praise and blame is the practice of humility, of being "right-sized."

In her groundbreaking research on learning and the brain, Carol S. Dweck, PhD, has found that certain kinds of praise can be harmful to children. If children are praised for being smart, they won't try as hard. They may feel they are being valued for an intrinsic quality over which they have no control. Because they don't want to look bad or lose that praise, they may avoid taking risks and never travel to the dynamic edge of their ability. It is more helpful to praise a child for their effort, helping them to develop the resilience to keep trying and growing.

One day, I called one of my students over to my desk. Though he was clearly very bright, I didn't feel that his work had measured up to his potential. I said quietly, "You know, it's the middle of the school year, and I don't think I've ever seen your best work."

He looked over one shoulder and then the other and whispered, "Nobody has!" At the end of the school year, he came to me and said sheepishly, "Now I know what it feels like to do my best."

Students can shift their attitude and come to understand that if they build their skills, they can be more successful. If they feel that it's okay to make mistakes and learn from them, cultivating resilience, they have the experience of slowly building toward a better effort and a better outcome. Dweck calls this a "growth mindset." I always had a sign in gold on the wall of my classroom: "In effort, there is joy. —Esteban Vicente, Spanish artist."

At the same time, we can break a child's heart with just a word if we shame them with humiliating criticism that attacks their very being. These wounds can create an impenetrable armor that can last well into adulthood.

In terms of praise and blame, it's important to listen to how we speak to ourselves. In Buddhism we honor right speech, but how do we speak to ourselves inside, where no one else can hear?

- Are you constantly judging yourself, meting out praise and blame for everything you do?
- Do you sometimes feel you are standing next to yourself with a clipboard and a checklist, constantly evaluating your performance?
- Do you hear the voice of a critical parent, teacher, or coach in your mind?
- Do you carry around the harsh judgment of an unforgiving partner?

One aspect of the Eight Worldly Dharmas is to lighten up with ourselves and others, to get off the tightrope between these opposites and just let things be. There is a place beyond praise and blame where, in a quiet moment, we can say to ourselves, "Don't worry, I know who I am." No matter what others may say or think about us, we know who we are. We can feel satisfaction in our effort, and we can gently recognize where we may have been wrong and make the appropriate correction. That's why we call it practice.

In the *Dhammapada*, the Buddha enjoins us, "Live in joy and freedom, even amongst those who are sick or troubled. Live in joy and a peaceful heart even among those in conflict. Quiet the mind and heart and find the sweet joy of living in the dharma."

---

## Reflections and Practices

- Sit quietly in your zazen posture for a few minutes, coming back to your breath.
- Remember times in your life when you've experienced praise or blame and how that affected you.
- Write about the kind of language you grew up with in your family of origin. Were you encouraged—or frequently chastised? Was there loving and affectionate talk? Were you exposed to harmful and judgmental speech about other groups of people? Were you often afraid? Are there patterns you may have inherited from your family that you would like to confront and change?

- How have the twin winds of success and failure shaped your life?
- Think about how you speak to yourself: Do you find yourself constantly criticizing yourself? Do you obsess over something that makes you feel ashamed?
- What would it be like to cultivate a loving inner witness, an inner voice that could console, help, and guide you as a trusted friend would? What would that voice sound like? Put your hand on your heart and take a few deep breaths. What would that voice like to say to you right now?

# 8

## The Eight Awarenesses of the Awakened Being

Our higher power is as close as our breath. Conscious aware-
ness of its presence strengthens us moment by moment. The
past is gone; today is full of possibilities. With each breath, I
will be aware of the strength at hand.

—Karen Casey, *Each Day a New Beginning*

IT IS SAID that the Mahaparinirvana Sutra was the last teaching
the Buddha gave before his death. Dogen Zenji, in his master-
work *Shobogenzo*, includes the translation of the Buddha's teach-
ing with the title "Hachidainingaku." Interestingly, this was also
apparently the last teaching Dogen gave before his own death in
1253.

The Eight Awarenesses of the Awakened Person include eight
realizations or awakenings that are available to us all:

- Having few desires
- Knowing how to be satisfied
- Enjoying serenity and tranquility
- Exerting meticulous effort
- Not forgetting right thought
- Practicing *samadhi*, a state of concentration or meditation
- Cultivating wisdom
- Avoiding idle talk

We can easily see that these aspects reflect and fold back on one another. If we have few desires, we know how to be satisfied. If we know how to be satisfied, we can better enjoy serenity and tranquility. If we can enjoy serenity and tranquility, we can exert our full effort. Part of right effort is right thought. With right thought we can meditate, and meditation helps us cultivate wisdom. If we are practicing wisdom, we won't waste so much time with idle talk.

Let's look a little more closely at these eight awarenesses.

If we have few desires, we will know how to be satisfied. Another way to think about this is that we can desire and be grateful for what we already have. The Buddha said, "Knowing how much to take of what one already has is called 'knowing how to be satisfied.' . . . You monks should contemplate knowing how to be satisfied if you wish to be liberated from suffering. The dharma of knowing how to be satisfied is the realm of riches, comfort, peace, and tranquility. Those who know how to be satisfied are happy and satisfied even when sleeping on the ground. Those who do not know how to be satisfied are not satisfied even when dwelling in a heavenly palace. Those who do not know how to be satisfied are poor even if they are wealthy, while those who know how to be satisfied are wealthy even though they have little. Those who do not know how to be satisfied and are always tempted by the five desires are consoled by those who know how to be satisfied. This is called 'knowing how to be satisfied.'"

There are a lot of lists in Buddhism. The five desires are wealth, sex, fame, food, and sleep. Right away we have a problem because included in these desires are things that we need to survive, that our species needs to survive. Sex is a natural human drive and a wonderful part of human life. Without food or sleep, we cannot live. Fame and wealth are perhaps extremes, but even the Buddha is famous, and some with wealth have done great things for others. Since the Buddha taught the value of living moderately, we can see that our lives and personalities can be impacted and distorted if we go to extremes in any of these five desires.

This teaching gets right to the heart of our ordinary everyday suffering, the suffering of always wanting things to be just a little different than they are. We tend to think that we could be truly happy, truly satisfied, if only we could make a few adjustments. Being able to be satisfied with what we already have, being able to have few desires, depends on whether we take our lives for granted, whether we take our gifts for granted, whether we can be grateful and appreciative of our lives just as they are.

Edward Espe Brown, a Zen priest whose *The Tassajara Bread Book* has brought many people to Zen Center, said to me once, "If you aren't happy with what you have, what makes you think you'd be happy with more?" If there is a silver lining to going through a difficult time, I think it's that when we are going through hardship, we may have the ability to find joy in seemingly small things. Just the sight of a delicate tree decorated with cherry blossoms can make us happy. Just a glass of cool water, a breath of fresh air, or the smile of a stranger can console us. We are grateful for simple things.

When someone you love is dying, all the things about them that you took for granted or that might have annoyed you suddenly seem so precious and dear. But those precious things are always close at hand if we can be open to them, if we can turn toward our own actual lives and appreciate what is right in front of us.

There is a saying in Zen: "Painted cakes don't satisfy." If we have some idea in our minds about what would finally satisfy us, if we crave some ideal that is always just out of reach, we can't enjoy the actual cake that is in front of us. The Buddha told us that our suffering begins with *tanha*, which literally means "thirst." There is no better example of this than the insatiability of addiction.

The Buddhist Wheel of Life pictures different realms. Hungry ghosts (*preta*) are pictured as beings with huge, empty stomachs; pinhole mouths; and necks so thin that they cannot swallow. A hungry ghost is one who is always looking outside themself for the new thing that will satisfy the craving within. Hungry ghosts are characterized by insatiable hunger and craving—with addiction, obsession, and compulsion.

In the world of addiction, we constantly seek outside ourselves for the cure for our insatiable yearning for relief. We are never truly satisfied by our addictions because they offer only an illusory, temporary relief. They don't give us what we really long for—connection, peace, a sense of being at home in the world. In fact, the longer we live in the realm of addiction, the more these comforts gradually recede into the distance, and we are bereft, sick, and alone.

When we sit in stillness and silence on the cushion or in the chair, we are seeing what it might be like to have few desires. We are learning how to be satisfied. We are enjoying serenity and tranquility. It requires meticulous effort to stay in our meditation posture and cultivate right thought. This continuous practice leads us to samadhi, the arising of wisdom. Naturally, when we are sitting in silence, we are avoiding idle talk. The Eight Awarenesses of the Awakened Person are all available to us in our sitting practice and in the work of recovery. We are practicing restraint rather than giving in to our habitual tendency to run off here and there seeking constant stimulation.

A friend of mine, newly sober, was sitting in a recovery meeting next to an "old-timer." Something the speaker said rubbed her the wrong way, and she stood up to leave. The old-timer took her gently by the wrist and pulled her down, saying, "We never leave meetings. We stay put." She later told me, "I learned how to sit still by staying in meetings, no matter what happened. I had to learn how to *stay* instead of running, the way I always had." Later, this thirst for peace and stillness brought her to Zen practice.

We may have come to practice and recovery after experiencing terrible suffering, after a long season in hell. But in practice and recovery we find the resources to cultivate satisfaction and contentment, to find a new freedom and a new happiness.

I have retired from teaching, and I will miss the shining faces of my third graders, who tumbled up to my door each morning like luminous beings. Once, when I was dealing with a very difficult situation in my life, I arrived at school to see one of my former students, Helena, waiting for me at the door with a wrapped present. I smiled and said, "For me?" and she replied, "Open it! Open it!"

It was a book called *F in Exams: The Very Best Totally Wrong Test Answers* by Richard Benson, a collection of student responses on various school tests. Here are a couple of examples:

QUESTION: *What was Sir Isaac Newton famous for?*
ANSWER: He invented gravity.
QUESTION: *Is the sun or the moon more important?*
ANSWER: The moon gives us light at night when we need it and the sun gives us light during the day when we don't need it, therefore, the moon is more important.

There was no way that Helena could have known that I needed cheering up that day, that her generous act of kindness would be something I would never forget. She reminded me how important it is to pass kindness along to others without knowing how it will land, where it will grow, who it might affect.

In that moment shared with Helena, I was flooded with some of the elements that can contribute to our peace and happiness, our serenity and tranquility: connection with other human beings, feeling appreciated and recognized, the healing qualities of laughter and humor, knowing to the core of my being that teaching children is meaningful work. Beyond that, I knew that it made her happy to find this perfect present for me and to give it to me, knowing that I would get a kick out of it. She was also saying to me, "I remember you."

In our recovery work, we enact the elements of happiness, of satisfaction and wisdom:

- Building a strong network of relationships
- Cultivating and expressing gratitude

- Taking responsibility for our actions and clearing up the past
- Discovering how to stay with difficult situations and emotions
- Finding that we can help others
- Learning how to avoid being too hungry, too angry, too lonely, or too tired
- Feeling that our lives matter, that we have something to offer
- Being able to enjoy the simple pleasures of everyday life

These things can give us real satisfaction rather than the "painted cakes," the simulated and artificial satisfaction of substance abuse or behavioral addictions. Stepping away from the big highs and lows of addiction, the drama and confusion, we turn toward our own lives. We can meditate with others and practice being satisfied with this present moment.

If we are torn up with bitterness and resentment, if we are caught in our anger and rage, then we are more likely to cause suffering to ourselves and others. Our practice and recovery offer us the "sacred pause," the ability to wait and breathe, and then to act with wisdom, serenity, and courage.

---

## Reflections and Practices

- Sit quietly in your zazen posture for a few minutes, coming back to your breath.
- Make a list of the things that make you feel peaceful and

joyful. Vow to conscientiously practice those things in your everyday life.

- Make a list of the simple things that give you satisfaction. Writing about them will help you remember to appreciate them. Choose some ordinary object that you live with every day but don't pay too much attention to and draw it. You may see it in a new way.

- What kinds of habits pull you away from joy and satisfaction? Make a list. Too much screen time? Obsessive worry? Chronic busyness at the expense of your inner life? Relationships that might be toxic or too consuming?

- Put all of this aside *right now* and take a walk, preferably in nature. As you walk, open your eyes, your ears, all your senses, and let yourself be bathed in the ever available and consoling present moment. Feel your feet on the ground. Feel the air on your face. Allow yourself to be grateful for this life.

# 9

## The Art of Losing

Life is like getting on a boat that is about to sail out to sea
and sink.

—Suzuki Roshi

KISO GOTAMI WAS THE WIFE of a wealthy man of Sravasti. One
morning, her son awoke with a high fever, and by nightfall, he
had died. Desperate with grief and unable to accept that her son
was dead, Kiso Gotami wrapped the tiny body in a blanket, as if
he were sleeping, and carried him with her everywhere, asking
everyone she met if they could bring her child back to life.

"You must go and see the Buddha," an old woman told her.
"He will help you."

Kiso Gotami walked to a nearby field where the Buddha was
teaching under the shade of a tree. She knelt before him with her
child's body cradled in her arms.

"Buddha, I have heard of your great wisdom and compassion.

Do you have some special magic that will bring my child back to me?"

The Buddha regarded the woman with kind eyes. "I can help you. But first, you must do something for me. You must go to the village and bring me a mustard seed. But the mustard seed must come from a family that hasn't been touched by death. Then come back to me."

So Kiso Gotami went from house to house, her dead child in her arms. She knocked at each door, but try as she might, she couldn't find a single household that didn't know death. She returned to the Buddha, finally understanding that death and grief are universal and part of human life, and she was able to place her son gently on a funeral pyre covered with beautiful flowers. From then on, she traveled with the Buddha as his disciple.

This is, in my words, the story of Kiso Gotami, a story that many of us know. But I have always felt that there is something missing from this story. In some versions I've come across, the Buddha tells her that he will bring her child back to life if she will return with a mustard seed from a family that hasn't known death. But how could a person with the Buddha's boundless compassion make such a cruel promise to someone who has lost a child? Can we bear the thought of Kiso Gotami searching ever more frantically for the elusive mustard seed that could revive her dead child?

No. I prefer to think the Buddha trusted that she would be invited in for a cup of tea at each home she visited. The people there would gently ask about her son, and she would remember him, the twinkle in his eyes, the things he loved. And they would tell Kiso Gotami about their loved ones who had died. There would be shared laughter and tears. Sitting with those people, she would find empathy and communion. When she rose to leave, she would be embraced and comforted. Yes, death and grief are universal, and so is our need to give and receive solace from others who have lost those whom they have loved.

This is also the jewel at the heart of recovery. Bringing our pain into the light and sharing it with others reminds us that we are not alone and that we have something to offer.

---

Kiso Gotami suffered a devastating loss that led her to the Buddha's path. But ordinary loss is part of everyday life. When I start losing things, it's a reminder for me to wake up. This kind of distraction tells me that something is amiss, that something is troubling me on a deeper level. In some profound way, I am not present for my life. Lao Tzu said, "Look well to this day, for this is life, the very life of life." When I start losing things, it is clear that I am elsewhere.

But sometimes we have to let go of things to make room for something new to come into our lives. Maybe that's why we lose things. Maybe it is a rehearsal for the letting go that is at the heart of practice and recovery. Letting go of the things we cling to, letting go of old ideas and habits. Letting go of what we have outgrown and then emerging, like a butterfly breaking free from its chrysalis.

Since I am a bit of a pessimist, I like to say that when one door closes, another door also closes. That the light at the end of the tunnel is the oncoming train. But there is something cathartic about taking inventory and getting rid of things we no longer need or use, of clothes we never wear, of broken appliances, of friends who don't respect or support us, of family members who frighten or abuse us. Letting go of old habits that threaten to slowly destroy us. Taking off the armor that no longer protects us but rather shields us from life and new experiences.

Sometimes it is only in hindsight that we realize some of the greatest losses in our lives were for the best. I wouldn't be the person I am without having loved Sam. And I could never have had the life I needed to live had I not left him behind. He moved to the Southwest and tried to get sober—and was, for various lengths of time. For years, long after I got sober, we continued to talk on the phone, often late at night when he was drunk or high. Sometimes he would tell me he was sober when it was clear that he was not. It was almost as if he needed me to think he was sober and somehow that would count for something.

Sam took his own life in 2020. When he died, a world died with him, and I miss talking to him about our travels and about the mysteries of life. I knew him my whole life; my father was his Cub Scout master when he was a little boy. Janet Malcolm wrote, "We are each of us an endangered species. When we die, our species disappears with us. Nobody like us will ever exist again." My friend John consoled me with the insight that, when someone we've loved dies, we feel the profound presence of an absence. When we love someone and lose them, they are still with us every day, yet it's still hard for me to think of a world without Sam.

Sadly, Sam's brother Chris had also ended his own life years before, out in the desert. Along the way, this disease has claimed many of the people I've loved. It is a disease that tells us we don't have a disease, a disease that wants to kill us.

As painful as it is to lose people and things we hold dear, the loss of them can offer signposts that we can take to heart, new vistas that we couldn't have imagined, capacities within ourselves that we might never have glimpsed. At the same time, we might be haunted by the memory of something or someone very precious that we let slip away without recognizing their value.

There is a famous Chinese fable called "A Blessing in Disguise" that relates to loss or letting go. This is my version of the story.

An old man lived on the plains of China with his only son, whom he loved more than all the world. The man and his son made a living by capturing wild horses and training and trading them.

One morning, the door to their stable was wide open, and they found that their most prized black stallion was missing. The neighbors, when they heard the news, came to offer their condolences. "What a shame that your most valuable horse has run away!" they said, shaking their heads in commiseration.

But to their surprise, the old man didn't chime in and agree with them. He merely said, with a twinkle in his eye, "We shall see."

A few days later, the stallion returned and trotting along beside him was a beautiful white mare. Again, the neighbors were at hand. "What great good fortune that you now have not one but two extraordinary horses. And one of them you got for free!"

Again, the old man, smiling, merely said, "We shall see."

Sure enough, bad luck came again. The old man's son was taming the mare when she startled and bucked, the son toppling to the ground where the horse fell on him, injuring his leg. From that day forward, he walked with a pronounced limp.

The neighbors visited again. "How unfortunate that your son has been injured by the white mare. Perhaps you should set her free before she does more damage!"

The old man replied, "We shall see."

An invading enemy swept into that part of the country, and all the young men for miles around were conscripted to serve in the army. But the old man's son was excused because of his injury.

"You are indeed very lucky that your son has not had to go off and risk his life in this terrible war," said the neighbors.

And the old man again replied, "We shall see."

When we lose something, when something goes wrong, when things don't go the way we want, when we don't get what we think we deserve, when our hearts are broken, we can't always see the blessings that might be embedded in loss and disappointment. When things seem to go well, we also don't know how they might ultimately turn out.

Practice and recovery encourage us to throw everything up in the air, all our cherished beliefs and limiting identities and ideas. And we only know that it is for the best because we see people around us who seem to be happy, joyous, and free, charting this new course of lives lived without dependence on substances or self-defeating behavior.

But we can also grieve for some aspects of our old way of life, since we are in the process of dying to our old selves. Elisabeth Kübler-Ross, in her groundbreaking book *On Death and Dying*, outlined what someone might go through when they face a life-threatening disease or the illness of someone they love:

- Denial
- Anger
- Bargaining
- Depression
- Acceptance

Looking back, I can see that I went through all those stages when I gave up alcohol and everything that went with it: the romance of it; the abandon it seemed to offer; my drinking companions; what William James, in his book *Varieties of Religious Experience*, characterized as the big YES that alcohol at first seems to promise.

I am fond of the wild woman I was. Because of alcohol, I was brave enough to travel through the Mideast in the 1970s and visit the opium dens of Afghanistan. Because of alcohol, I could sing in bars and in front of large groups of people. I could dance all night and talk to anyone. I could do all kinds of crazy things, take all kinds of risks, and feel more alive and freer than I ever had before. Because of alcohol, I could uproot myself and travel alone to Alaska and start a new life. But because of alcohol, I ended up in a cabin in the snow in the Alaskan winter contemplating suicide. In Alaska, I traveled to the heart of darkness. In that cabin, I had a moment of awakening. I sensed within me a glimmer of hope that if I stuck around, there might be more abundant life at the end of the long dark tunnel, that maybe there was something about the way I was living, the way I was dancing with the darkness, that brought me to such a defeated and terrifying place.

I came back to San Francisco and began to come back to life, but to do that, I began to understand that I couldn't bring alcohol along with me. I went through all the stages of loss and grief as I started the long process of moving beyond alcohol:

- The *denial* that I was a "real" alcoholic
- The *bargaining*—"If I just get out of this one alive, I'll never do this again."

- Living in a fog of *anger* and resentment
- The *depression* that goes hand in hand with alcohol because it *is* a depressant.
- And finally, the *acceptance* that necessitated conceding to my inmost self that I was an alcoholic and couldn't drink like other people

I who have died am alive again today.

—e. e. cummings

Losing alcohol, which had been my companion off and on for many years, was a kind of death, and with it there was grief. There was loss. There was losing. What I got in return for that loss was riches beyond compare. Yet there is a kind of death and grief that goes along with this upheaval in our lives, this shifting of tectonic plates that demands much from us. *All* is not lost. We find that, no matter what our story is, we have something to offer others. In a way, we don't give up that old way of life; we transform it through identification with other suffering people and that is truly a kind of alchemy. We find that the very places where we are broken and grieving are the places where we connect with other people.

It is in "dying" that we are born into a new life of recovery.

---

## Reflections and Practices

- Sit quietly in your zazen posture for a few minutes, coming back to your breath.

- If you are new to recovery, or if you have been sober for a while and think it might be helpful, write a letter to your addiction. Tell your addiction the things you loved about it, the things that disturbed you about it, the things that harmed you and other people. Tell some funny stories about it. Explain that it is time for you to move on but that you will never forget where you came from, lest you repeat it.
- Consider the five stages of grief. Can you remember going through these stages in relation to your addiction? Share these memories with a trusted friend.
- Have you lost anyone to addiction? Choose one or two people and write them a letter. Tell them how you are doing; tell them what you miss about them and what you would have wished for them. Though you won't be able to deliver it to them, you can deliver it to your own heart and hold your memories dear. If you have a home altar, you can put their pictures and your letters there.

# 10

## Life Is But a Dream

Row, row, row your boat
Gently down the stream,
Merrily, merrily, merrily, merrily,
Life is but a dream.

—Traditional children's rhyme

IKKYU WAS A CLEVER BOY who lived in Japan a very long time ago. He slept in a corner of the meditation hall in a temple in Kyoto, and his teacher was a very stern Zen master. The boy's job was to sweep the entrance to the temple in the morning and evening and to make tea for his master and for the guests who came to visit the temple.

In Japan, tea ceremony is a special art, and Ikkyu's master had spent many years studying the art of tea. There was one teacup that he especially liked. It was a mysterious shade of blue, with the image of a graceful goldfish that looked like it was swimming in deep water.

One day, Ikkyu rose with the temple bells and swept the path as he did each day. While the monks were sitting zazen in the meditation hall, he built a small fire in the hearth to heat water for morning tea. He wanted to please his teacher, so he stood on a three-legged stool and reached up to a high shelf where the special goldfish teacup was kept.

Uh oh! The stool began to wobble and Ikkyu fell off, crashing to the floor. He jumped up and brushed himself off, unharmed. But the teacup, the very special teacup that his master loved so dearly, had broken into a dozen pieces. Ikkyu quickly picked up his broom, swept up the pieces, and wrapped them in a red cloth, tying the four corners together.

When zazen was over and the ringing of the bells and the chanting of the monks had faded away, Ikkyu heard his master's footsteps coming toward him in the hallway. The mischievous boy hid the small red bundle behind his back.

When the master came into the room, Ikkyu was waiting for him. "Master," he asked innocently, tilting his small face up to his teacher, "why must people die?"

The master was fond of the boy, and his face broke into a patchwork of wrinkles as he smiled down at him. He laid a gentle hand on Ikkyu's head. "Because, my boy, that is the way things are. That is the way of life. Everything that *is* must someday come to an end."

"Master," said the boy, holding out the red bundle containing the broken teacup. "I'm sorry to say that it was time for your favorite teacup to come to an end."

The old master couldn't help it. He threw his head back and laughed out loud. "Let's have a cup of tea!" he said. And he took two teacups from the shelf.

Ikkyu grew up to be a poet, a flute player, and a Zen master. He was also famous as a master of the tea ceremony.

—Adapted from an ancient Japanese tale

---

The great truth of impermanence is always with us.

The thirteenth-century Persian Sufi poet Farid al-Din Attar of Nishapu told the fable of an ancient king who gathered a group of wise men around him: "Please give me some medicine that will keep me from being too happy when I am happy and too sad when I am sad. Give me some words that will be true in all circumstances."

The wise men withdrew and murmured to one another. The next day, they presented the king with a ring. Engraved on the ring were the words "This, too, shall pass."

This verse appears in the great Mahayana Buddhist text the Diamond Sutra:

Like a falling star, like a bubble in a stream,
Like a flame in the wind, like frost in the sun,
Like a flash of lightning or a passing dream—
So should you understand the conditioned world.

Japanese culture is rooted in the contemplation of beauty against a background of impermanence. Pico Iyer, in his book *Autumn Light*, cites the celebration of spring cherry blossoms, which emerge and pass away with their fleeting beauty. Then in the fall, families picnic at the foot of trees and walk among them, admiring their flaming red and golden leaves, which will soon flutter to the ground. Pico writes, "We cherish things, Japan has always known, precisely because they cannot last; it's their frailty that adds sweetness to their beauty. . . . Autumn poses the question we all have to deal with: How to hold on to the things we love even though we know that we and they are dying. How to see the world as it is yet find light within that truth."

In her book *Start Where You Are*, Pema Chödrön, an American teacher of Tibetan Buddhism, shares some practice slogans or sayings to help cultivate *bodhicitta*, the quality of our awakened heart, the compassion, openness, and clarity that are available to all of us when we open our hearts to one another without defense or armor. The first slogan she suggests is, "Regard all dharmas as dreams." This echoes the words of the Diamond Sutra that remind us to regard as impermanent the nature of this conditioned world.

The word *dharma* refers to the Buddha's teachings on the nature of reality. Everything that we experience is dharma, the truth, the Way, the path. The discriminating mind wants to pick and choose: this is good, this is bad, this is worthwhile, this is a waste of time, I like this, I don't like that. But with an open heart, we can regard everything that arises as part of the teaching.

Whether someone is helpful toward us or not, we can include them in our practice. Perhaps the people and events that are the most irritating or challenging are the most beneficial to us, because without them we might not be encouraged to go beyond our limited point of view.

We often speak of "living in the present moment," but by the time we realize that we've heard the sound of a baby laughing, smelled a fragrance, seen a redwood tree, tasted an apple, or felt a feeling, it is already gone. It is already a memory, like the light from the stars we see today that left those stars thousands of years ago.

If someone says something that offends me, that hurts my feelings, by the time my particular personal constellation of past experiences get together and decide that I've been offended, it is already over. In this sense, everything that happens to us is a memory of something that is already over, just like a dream.

This may be a difficult idea for us to understand because when we come to recovery, we come because we long for real life, not for the wispy dreams we may have chased in the past that were ultimately unsatisfying. We may feel that we've already spent years in the fog of addiction, which at first promised more vivid life and in the end became a mindless repetition. We want to wake up from that bad dream and be truly alive.

This metaphor is most helpful when it is grounded in practice, which roots us in the physicality of everyday life. Against the background of impermanence, the Buddha invites us to "joyfully participate in the sorrows of the world." (I'd love to tell you that I read this in the *Dhammapada*, but it's something one of Tony Soprano's girlfriends says to him when they are walking through the Bronx Zoo.)

When we sit, we follow our breath. It comes and goes. Our thoughts arise and fall away. Sometimes we follow them for a little while, caught by an image, a story, a regret, and then we remember our breath and come back to the present moment. We see that our feelings come and go, that our thoughts come and go, just like our breath. In this simple practice of *staying*, we experience the truth of impermanence.

Without impermanence, our children couldn't grow up; we would not be able to change, to right social wrongs, to make amends for our transgressions, to witness the sunrise and, later, sunset. To step onto the path of recovery.

Recently, I was plunged into worry about someone I love. I thought of the teaching "Regard all dharmas as dreams." As soon as this situation was resolved, my worry evaporated. This pervasive worry, which had seemed so tangible, like a big demon in the room, just blew away like a dream. Worry didn't help me or the person I was worrying about, but making a big pot of minestrone soup did.

It may be helpful to consider this whenever we take ourselves too seriously or find ourselves getting swept away by strong emotions. We can try it and see if we have a more lighthearted feeling, an opening up, a little less self-clinging.

The other side of things is that there's this pesky material plane we need to take care of. If we cling to this idea that life is like a dream, we may forget to pay our bills or sweep the floor or make the bed. So, there's that. But we can call this dreamlike quality to mind when we become too enmeshed in the temporary dramas of the everyday.

To come back to the notion of someone hurting our feelings, by the time we realize we are hurt, it is already over, but we often indulge our very human tendency to nurse that wound, to make it solid and immovable, to replay it, to tell other people about it, to think of what we could have said, or go back to the person and say it. We can create a whole story about this event that can haunt us and wake us up at night. A passing feeling or thought can assume a kind of solidity as we recreate it and keep it alive. Why do we do this when we know it makes us miserable? I think we hold on to these things with the misguided idea that by doing so we are standing up for ourselves, protecting ourselves. We would help ourselves more if we could learn to let go more. This doesn't mean that it is okay for others to abuse us. But we don't need to limit or define ourselves by the ways in which we have been hurt. The things that hurt us or haunt us don't last forever. They don't have much reality without our strange need to keep feeding them and keeping them alive.

We learn in recovery about the "deliberate manufacture of misery." When we nurse our resentments and keep them alive, we are manufacturing misery, prolonging and making more solid our own suffering rather than letting go and seeing things as a dream, noticing that they are impermanent.

I'm not talking about affirmations or looking at the bright side or counting our blessings. Practice isn't about turning away from or stuffing our feelings.

First, we feel the pain, we recognize the hurt, we understand that if our heart is open, it will sometimes get bruised. Then we accept ourselves and our feelings, exactly where we are, without judgment. We take time to notice the size and shape and texture of our feelings. We might even have intimations that these feelings are deeply rooted in other experiences that preceded this one. Finally, we find ways to nurture ourselves and to heal our ragged and distracting emotions, by ourselves or with the help of our dharma friends.

I have found, in experimenting with this teaching, that life is "like frost in the sun, like a flash of lightning or a passing dream," a feeling of lightness and fresh air comes in. This is a tangible way of practicing with impermanence.

In his great poem "Genjokoan," Dogen Zenji said, "Flowers fall and weeds spring up." Things that we wish would last forever die, and the things we fear or hate flourish. This is also at the root of our suffering, always wishing that things could be different than they are. We forget, when we are in the pit of despair, that weeds also fall and flowers also spring up.

Where does this leave us as recovering people? Though I practiced Zen Buddhism without drinking for the first five years and then drank off and on for the next five, I didn't find the tools that recovery has given me to confront my past actions. When called to mind, the residue of the past could threaten to lead me back to the illusory comfort of alcohol.

Life may be like a dream; we may be living from moment to moment in an eternal present, but until we look at, take responsibility for, and clear up our past, we may be destined to repeat it. There is a deadly repetition and monotony to addiction, and in many families, it is manifested through generation after generation. When I visited Ireland, I was so grateful that I and other family members have been granted the grace to change this seemingly endless pattern of alcoholism that has been passed down in my family going all the way back to the British Isles. I was so pleased when I was asked to share my story at a meeting on the Dingle Peninsula.

When we step onto the path of practice and recovery, we live with this paradox, fully inhabiting the present moment while also recognizing how important it is to confront the past and transform it. Until we have done that, with the help of our spiritual friends, we are not free to fully live this present.

We live in both realities: this dreamlike world where each thing that occurs is already a memory, already gone, and the need to honestly take stock of our history and redeem it where possible. Atonement for the past frees us to live a different future. Unless we do the work of exploration and remorse that is offered to us in our recovery work, it can have the ability to bring us down. We don't do this work just for ourselves or even for our family, though those things are important. We do them because the world needs us to bring ourselves fully to life so that we can live and be lived for the benefit of all beings: our Bodhisattva Vow.

We make this wholehearted effort to sit still, to follow our breath, to live one day at a time. To open our hearts and take ourselves a little more lightly, meeting each moment as it arises, meeting all beings as they present themselves to us.

We have greater freedom to do this when we have done the hard work of atonement, when we have done the work that liberates us to live an awakened life.

---

## Reflections and Practices

Sit quietly in your zazen posture for a few minutes, coming back to your breath.

### WAKING UP

Every day think as you wake up, "Today I am fortunate to have woken up. I am alive. I have a precious human life, and I am not going to waste it. I am going to use all my energies to develop myself, to expand my heart out to others, to achieve enlightenment for the benefit of all beings."

—His Holiness the Fourteenth Dalai Lama

- It is very helpful to develop a morning routine that will help you set and realize your intention for the day. Sitting zazen, chanting the Loving-Kindness Sutra, reading recovery literature, previewing the day and how you wish to enter and live it. What is your morning routine?
- At the end of the day, you can review how it went. Is there anything nagging at you, some word or deed that you need to revisit and amend? Did you treat others kindly, as you would want to be treated? Did you honor the precepts today? Though each day passes by and is gone, sometimes the residue of some unskillful word or action can follow us and stay with us until we take care of it.

# 11

---

# Seeing in the Dark

You can hold back from the suffering of the world. You have
free permission to do so, and it is in accordance with your
nature. But perhaps this very holding back is the one suffering
you could have avoided.

—Franz Kafka

A STORY FROM our Western tradition teaches us something
about the journey into darkness and the return to light, about the
struggle toward freedom. Each person's life brings them in and
out of the darkness, and if we go into the darkness with our eyes
wide open, as we do in our work of recovery, we can emerge bear-
ing jewels. This is my version of the ancient tale.

Demeter was the goddess of the earth and the harvest, and she
lived with the other immortals on Mount Olympus. Her daughter,
Persephone, was the apple of her eye, and when Demeter would
come down to the earth to tend to the growing crops, she would

often bring her daughter with her. Together, they would dance and play in the green fields of the world.

Persephone glowed with a golden light. Whenever anyone laid eyes on her, they smiled, and where she walked, flowers sprang up at her feet. Hades, the god of the underworld, wanted her for his bride, and he watched and he waited.

One spring day, when Demeter and her daughter were dancing under the blossoming trees with the earthly nymphs, Persephone wandered off into a far field, picking flowers. Hades saw his chance and came roaring up from the underworld in his dark chariot. He seized the beautiful, young Persephone and descended again into the world below. There, on a hillside overlooking the valley, he had her sit beside him on a jewel-encrusted throne, and together they could look down and see the dead coming across the River Styx, each with a gold coin on their tongue to pay the boatman. On the banks of the river, the deeds of their lives were judged by Rhadamanthus, and they were sent to live in peace and light in the Elysian Fields or confined to Hades's dark kingdom for eternity.

Meanwhile, Demeter searched in vain for her daughter, and when she heard a rumor that Hades had abducted her, she was grief-stricken and furious. She went to Zeus, the king of the gods, and said that the earth would lie fallow and lifeless until her daughter was returned to her. Zeus sent Hermes with a message to Hades to return the girl at once.

But when Hermes descended into the underworld and delivered his message, Hades's gardener stepped forward and silently held out a ruptured pomegranate. Three of the jewel-like, ruby-red seeds were missing. In her grief, Persephone had absentmindedly

eaten three seeds from the only fruit to be found in Hades's king-
dom. Once one eats the food of Hades, one must stay there for-
ever, but because she had eaten only three of the seeds, this curse
was softened: she was able to return to Mount Olympus with her
mother, but she had to come back to Hades for three months out of
each year. That is why, when Persephone descends into the under-
world, the crops of the earth are dormant as Demeter waits anx-
iously for her daughter's return.

This can be our story of recovery—that we can descend into
the dark and emerge awakened and able to live for the benefit of
all beings.

By going to the dark places where we traveled in our addic-
tion, we are able to align ourselves with all suffering beings. We
are better able to cultivate compassion for ourselves and others,
better able to reach out to others with help and sustenance. Bet-
ter able to take action against injustice, prejudice, and hatred. To
stand tall with others in the causes in which we believe.

Each of us in this human life will suffer some time in a dark,
hellish place. Whether we want to or not, each of us spends our
season in hell. Practice and recovery are not separate from those
dark places. We turn toward the darkness and practice with it,
not regretting the past or trying to forget it, but rather, using the
energy and wisdom of our story as a kind of compost for growth.
We turn toward the darkness that we inhabited, and by our own-
ing it, it ceases to own us. As the poet Theodore Roethke put it, "In
a dark time, the eye begins to see . . ."

Telling our story of recovery is like Persephone returning to
Hades for part of the year. We know that by sharing our dark-
est secrets, they lose their hold on us, remind us where we came
from, and give us the chance to help other suffering people. Par-

adoxically, telling our story and hearing other people's stories renew our recovery.

We stay with this vulnerable heart of sadness that comes along with being alive instead of trying to fix it or make it better. This soft, sad heart is what connects us to one another.

Susan Barry, a neurobiologist, had vision problems as an infant, and in her forties, through extensive therapy and training, she learned how to see in three dimensions rather than just two. When Terry Gross, on the NPR radio show *Fresh Air*, asked her to share something thrilling that she's been able to see since learning how to see in this new way, she said, "I guess I would have to say trees. Over and over again, something that I see every day as I walk to work, a canopy of trees over my head. The branches reaching out toward you, where the different branches enclose palpable pockets of space. I sometimes find myself admiring those spaces in a tree and actually walking and immersing myself in those pockets of space. I used to see a snowfall as a flat sheet at just a little distance in front of me. I didn't feel I was part of the snowfall. Now, when I watch the snow coming down from the sky, each snowflake is in its own space, and there are volumes of space between each snowflake. Each snowflake produces its own unique, three-dimensional dance, and I feel immersed in the snowfall and part of it."

This is a woman who doesn't take her vision for granted. In her book *Fixing My Gaze*, she talks about the neuroplasticity of the brain, that we aren't "stuck" with the way we see and experience the world but can, with training, change.

Her story reminds us that, when we come through a dark, difficult time, the world can seem a little brighter, a little fuller. That we can look at something as ordinary as trees and revel in wonder because, for some of us, it is a miracle that we are alive to see. And in honor of Susan Berry, after I heard her story, I lay on the grass looking up at trees, appreciating their marvelous three-dimensionality.

Just as Susan Barry retrained her eyes to see differently, our practice and recovery can produce a profound transformation in the way we react to the world. Though we don't have much control over events around us, we can change the way we react to them— we can change the way we see them. We can emerge from the dark bearing jewels, more prepared to help other beings and to have a well-earned compassion for ourselves.

When we feel overwhelmed by the chaos and troubles of the world, we can pick one or two ways to "shine one corner of the world," as Suzuki Roshi put it, ways that we can be of service without reservation. We can even approach with love and compassion the parts of ourselves that we might want to reject, going into the darkness with open eyes and looking for the jewels.

And we can always stop and look up at the trees.

---

## Reflections and Practices

- Sit quietly in your zazen posture for a few minutes, coming back to your breath.

Keep reminding yourself: Every time you read a book, or take a class, or write a poem, or watch a sunset, or teach something to a child. Every time you love someone or find something beautiful. Every time you advance, however incrementally, the cause of intelligent civilization. Every time you pump a little warmth into this big, cold universe, you illustrate the real reason we are here. You solve the mystery. You don't need to ask anymore. You know the answer.

—Joel Achenbach, in his farewell letter
upon leaving the *San Francisco Chronicle*

- Make a list of some of the actions that you have taken to make the world a little better, to "pump a little warmth into this big, cold universe."
- What abilities, skills, and strengths have you discovered in recovery?
- What talents, interests, and activities do you want to develop further now that you have the gift of recovery?

# 12

---

# Crossing Over

## THE SIX PARAMITAS

Check your ordinary thoughts of greed, hatred, and ignorance, and return to your original pure mind.

—Yamada Roshi

AS WE FIND OUR WAY through the world as recovering people, we can ask ourselves, "Will my words and actions lead to greater happiness and freedom or to further suffering for myself and others?" We may have once believed that freedom meant doing whatever we wanted, without a thought for the consequences. But the principles of recovery teach us that, to experience true freedom, we need to cultivate an ethical life so we aren't undermined and distracted by guilt, shame, and remorse. We learn to take the needs and feelings of others into our hearts and imagine how they see things so that we can be agents of peace in the world.

Buddhist precepts teach us *what not to do*: not to kill, not to take what is not given, not to lie, not to misuse sexuality, not to intoxicate the mind or body of self or others—all the things we had to make amends for if we wanted to have some peace. You might say, as you survey past behavior, that addiction is the opposite of the precepts.

The Six Perfections, or Paramitas, are teachings that tell us *what we can do* to promote freedom and peace. These are qualities that we can study, focus on, and cultivate, actions we can take that help us drop our ordinary thoughts of greed, hatred, and ignorance and return to our original pure mind. In Sanskrit, *paramita* means "perfection," or "crossing over to the other shore," the shore of peace, of nonfear, of liberation.

I've learned to distrust perfectionism because I've found that it leads to procrastination, self-doubt, and paralyzing self-judgment. But the Six Perfections awaken in us a kind of natural wholesomeness, a commonsense path to greater ease and joy. Please don't worry too much about the word *perfection*; we don't have to wait around to become perfect. We can cross over to the other shore in every moment. As Thich Nhat Hanh puts it in *The Heart of the Buddha's Teaching*, "We can look at our anger, depression, and suffering, breathe deeply and smile."

These are the Six Paramitas:

*Dana*—generosity
*Shila*—ethical behavior
*Ksanti*—patience
*Virya*—effort
*Dhyana*—meditation
*Prajna*—wisdom

The paramitas are inseparable from one another, a continuum of life-affirming qualities. When you are practicing one of them, you are practicing all of them. And though Prajna Paramita (wisdom) is listed last, in Mahayana Buddhism it is described as the Mother of all Buddhas, the ground from which all practice flows. We cultivate these qualities without expecting anything in return. As Pema Chödrön puts it in *When Things Fall Apart*, "When we are training in the art of peace, we are not given any promises that, because of our noble intentions, everything will be okay. In fact, there are no promises of fruition at all. Instead, we are encouraged to look deeply at joy and sorrow, at laughing and crying, at hoping and fearing, at all that lives and dies. We learn that what truly heals is gratitude and tenderness."

## Dana Paramita: The Perfection of Generosity

To give is nonattachment, just not to attach to anything is to give.

—Suzuki Roshi

We might say that generosity is the opposite of self-centered fear, as much of an action as a state of mind. When we practice generosity, we are cultivating and offering an openhearted feeling toward the whole world, learning to let go of, or hold more lightly, our own limited view of self and others.

In *When Things Fall Apart*, Pema Chödrön comments, "The causes of aggression and fear begin to dissolve by themselves when we move past the poverty of holding back. The basic idea of generosity is to train in thinking bigger, to do ourselves the world's biggest favor and stop cultivating our own schemes."

This is a realm beyond the tightly held views, preferences, prejudices, and opinions to which we think we need to hold to continue being who we think we are. Thinking bigger lets in some fresh air and sunlight and allows room for our own mistakes and those of other people. Perhaps the greatest gift we can give one another is simply being fully present. Whatever peace and stability we can cultivate in ourselves is also a gift we can give away.

Here are some practices we learn in recovery that awaken our generosity:

- Showing up for a meeting
- Speaking to the person next to us
- Making coffee before and folding chairs after a meeting
- Sharing our story in an honest, openhearted way
- Helping others get started on the path of recovery
- Doing any kind of service
- Being fully present for another suffering person
- Allowing others to help us and thereby deepen their own recovery

The generosity that is awakened in recovery flows from humility, the understanding that we are no greater or less than anyone else and that each of us has something to offer. Generosity and humility are mixed up with gratitude: when we cultivate gratitude, we naturally feel more openhearted and generous, able to help and be present for others who are in darkness because we have lived in that darkness ourselves. This is not a self-righteous generosity, but generosity tempered by humility. The word *humility* is related to the word *humus*, or "earth," and means that we are right-sized and close to the earth.

One day, on my way home from morning zazen, there was a man sleeping near the front door of Zen Center. "I can make him some breakfast!" I thought to myself and hurried up the street to my place, brimming with self-satisfaction. I scrambled some eggs and put them, with some buttered toast, on a paper plate and made some coffee and poured it into a paper cup. Feeling quite pleased with myself, I went back down the street and up the steps of Zen Center, where the man was just waking up.

I said gently, "I've made you some breakfast."

Unimpressed, he looked at my offering, looked up at me, and said, "Ya got any *salt?*"

His reaction made me realize that I was expecting something in return for my generosity, validation that I am a good and generous person. I mumbled something about having salted the eggs and made my way home, a slightly humbler version of myself. When we give so that we can get something back, are we truly practicing generosity?

We can't be generous when we are trapped in self-centered fear. One of the greatest gifts of our recovery work is to face our fears. We may have been blind to the way that fear has warped our behavior and relationships in the past. Freedom from fear is freedom from the bondage of self. To grow in recovery, we need to loosen up and let go of old ideas. We confront our old behavior and make amends to those we have harmed. When we are flooded with gratitude for our recovery, our self-centered fear begins to melt away, and our generosity can bloom.

In *The Compass of Pleasure: How Our Brains Make Fatty Foods, Orgasm, Exercise, Marijuana, Generosity, Vodka, Learning, and Gambling Feel So Good*, David Linden, a professor of neuroscience at the Johns Hopkins University School of Medicine, explains how addiction hijacks the pleasure centers of the brain, causing the user to indulge in more and more of their substance or behavior of choice just to feel "normal." Linden's work highlights how recovering addicts, to sustain sobriety, need to develop wholesome and healthful activities that give the mind/body a biochemical burst of pleasure similar to that of their addictions. Studies show that when subjects perform generous acts—volunteering their time; engaging in charitable giving, even anonymously—a pleasurable dopamine release, similar to physical exercise or using substances like wine or marijuana, occurs. Not that we should be generous so we can get a dopamine rush!

In his discussion of generosity in *The Heart of Buddha's Teaching*, Thich Nhat Hanh suggests that generosity is cultivated in our mindful sitting, in following our breath and developing peace, freedom, and stability: "The greatest gift we have to offer others is our true presence."

He goes on to list things we can give that can't be wrapped up and tied with a ribbon: our freedom, our freshness, our understanding, and plenty of space for people to be exactly who they are. He offers this *gatha*, a verse to bring us back to peace: Breathing in, I see myself as still water; breathing out, I reflect things as they are.

Once, in our morning circle, I asked my third graders, "What was the best present you ever received?" The kids mentioned computer games, toys, sports equipment. But a girl who had been adopted from overseas by her American mother smiled and said, "My mom!"

## Reflections and Practices

Make a note in your journal as you watch generosity arise in your daily life or as you watch it get snuffed out because of causes and conditions:

- What inspires your generosity?
- Do certain people bring out your natural generosity?
- Did you learn generosity in your family of origin? How was it practiced?
- How has recovery affected your generosity?
- What obstructs your generosity?
- A friend told me that her father advised her, "Never ignore a generous impulse." The next time a generous impulse arises, see what it feels like to act on it rather than ignore it.
- What does it feel like to smile at people you pass on the sidewalk?
- Thank everybody! The person who delivers your mail, the lifeguard at the swimming pool, the person behind the desk. Being grateful to others is a way to cultivate our own generosity. It just feels good.
- Choose a difficult person in your life and respond to them with generosity, warmth, and an open heart—no matter what their reaction might be. This will drive them crazy.

## Shila Paramita: The Perfection of Ethical Conduct

Zen study is character change.

—Yamada Roshi

A teacher gathered her students together and said, "Why should we have to go out begging for food? Let others do the work for us. If you see someone coming down the path with a basket of fruit or a bag of rice, surprise them and take it from them. But make sure no one sees you."

All of the teacher's students went off to see if they could hide behind a tree until someone came by with some food worth taking. All of her students but one.

"Teacher," said the student, "you know I love and respect you. I would do anything you ask of me. But I don't understand your teaching. You say I can take the food if no one sees me."

"That's right," said the teacher.

"Teacher, that's impossible! Because *I* can always see me."

The teacher smiled, "You alone have understood my teaching."

—Adapted from a Jataka Tale

We can engage in *shila*, ethical conduct, by living in accordance with Buddhist precepts. Many of us don't like the word *discipline* because we associate it with losing something—a part of ourselves, our own spontaneity. It may be a word that we associate with punishment received as a child. But we know enough about discipline to know that simply by admitting we are addicted to substances or self-defeating behaviors, and taking the steps to arrest our disease, a world of freedom is available to us. Maybe there are other things that we can refrain from that will also increase our liberation. Discipline takes on a different meaning when it comes from the inside out, when we act out of our inmost desire to be the person we are meant to be.

This is a new kind of freedom—the freedom of restraint. In zazen practice, not moving just because we want to, but sitting still. Following our breath rather than letting our thoughts and preoccupations run away with us. Practicing moderation and mindfulness in our lives. Thinking before we speak and asking ourselves if these words will lead to greater happiness and freedom or to further suffering. These mindful practices, rather than restricting us, enable us to let go more fully and to open up to the present moment. They help free us from painful, habitual patterns.

The words *disciple* and *discipline* come from Latin roots meaning "pupil" and "to learn." If we practice discipline with compassion for self and others, we can open up to gentleness, to honesty, to letting go. This is not about becoming a better person, a person we are not yet worthy of being, but of returning to our true nature, our true home, our "original pure mind." This is being the person we are meant to be.

Eijun Linda Cutts, senior dharma teacher at San Francisco Zen Center's Green Gulch Farm and my teacher, pointed out, "Long before there were precepts, there was the One Mind, which is our true nature. It's not that we practice the precepts in order to *become*. We practice the precepts because that's who we are. . . . When we make this kind of effort, there is a response in our lives. This is being in relationship with our true self. The precepts are Zen practice, and zazen mind is every single instance of our lives, every thought is an expression of One Mind. Every single thing is important, is worthy of our attention. Being in true relationship means to care for and dedicate each moment of my life to caring for everyday life."

We might say that ethical conduct, or shila, is doing the right thing even when no one else is looking. This is not a moral judgment nor a standard imposed from outside, but a sense of rightness, of beneficial speech and action that comes to us through our own practice and through the inner work and work we do with others in recovery.

The Ten Grave Precepts of Buddhism are:

- Not to kill
- Not to take what is not given
- Not to lie
- Not to intoxicate the mind or body of self or others
- Not to misuse sexuality
- Not to slander others
- Not to praise self at the expense of others
- Not to be avaricious
- Not to harbor ill will
- Not to abuse the Three Treasures—Buddha, Dharma, and Sangha

These precepts, a commonsense guide to conduct, are more available to us with the clarity that comes with recovery. We develop an intuitive sense of the difference between what is right and what is not right and often notice a physical and mental sensation of unease or discomfort when our thoughts, words, and deeds are not in alignment with our deepest intention.

When we behave or speak in an unskillful way, there is a kind of residue or stickiness that follows us until we clean up the damage we have done. Practice and recovery give us a practical way to be true to our intention to live as the person we are meant to be. We can be in conscious contact with our daily lives, waking up to the consequences of our thoughts, words, and deeds.

We can look at the precepts literally or in a broader way, with greater nuance. Perhaps we wouldn't kill one of our fellow creatures—but do our individual choices affect the environment in negative ways? Perhaps we wouldn't lie—but do we withhold important aspects of ourselves from our partner? Perhaps we wouldn't steal—but do we rob time from a friend by monopolizing our conversations with our own obsessive preoccupations?

In my disease, I used to say and do things that made me uncomfortable. This often caused me to turn toward my addictions for comfort. Alcohol tends to inhibit the executive functioning of the brain and causes us to act from that organ's more primitive regions. When drinking, I'd often do and say things that made me feel guilty and ashamed—and the cycle continued.

The Buddha encourages us to develop our compassion (*karuna*) and wisdom (*prajna*). To cultivate compassion, we turn our attention toward the way we interact with others and with the world. The precepts help us cultivate an ethical life, as well as compassion toward self and others. No spiritual life is possible without looking at and adjusting our behavior so it is in line with our values. In order to achieve and maintain our sobriety, we need to shine a light on our past, on things we said, on lies we told, on harmful actions taken in anger and resentment. It can be helpful to appraise our behavior through the lens of the precepts.

Several of the precepts focus on speech. A disciple of the Buddha doesn't lie, doesn't slander others, doesn't harbor ill will, doesn't praise self at the expense of others. The other precepts can also be applied to speech. A disciple of the Buddha doesn't kill, and we can kill another person's joy and enthusiasm with a harsh word or cruel attack. We can abuse the Three Treasures by gossiping about other sangha members.

Lying is often connected with negative sexual behavior, codependence, and substance abuse, because these are things we seem to need to lie about. Lying is a constant companion when we act out in our disease. There's an old saying: "How can you tell if an addict is lying? Their lips are moving." I sometimes think that lying is a misguided impulse to spin a web of secrecy and privacy around ourselves so no one else knows exactly who we are. While we may have needed this privacy at one time to protect ourselves in our family of origin, perhaps now we can move toward greater transparency.

Slandering others, speaking ill of them to anyone who will listen, seems to make us feel better than they are and to shore up our wavering self-esteem. But it erodes other people's trust in us, because if I gossip with you about someone else, you may suspect that I'll gossip with someone else about you. I can also slander myself by denigrating myself with negative self-talk, either in my own mind or in the way I represent myself to others.

Harboring ill will is indulging in resentment and self-justified anger through our thoughts, our speech, and our actions. We perpetuate our suffering by obsessing about some event, often long past, over which we have little control. Here is Pema Chödrön's astute observation: "Holding a grudge is like eating rat poison and expecting the rat to die." The mental and physical effects of harboring ill will are well known.

Praising self at the expense of others is more of the same. Gossiping unkindly about others is a kind of praising self at the expense of others because we are implying that we would never be like those other awful people.

Practice is the activity of bringing our full awareness to our lives. We don't need to feel bad when we notice that we still indulge in these behaviors, but we can start observing these things in ourselves, noticing that they don't create happiness and peace, and let them gradually lessen or slip away.

We can study ourselves in a loving way and begin to wonder what we get out of negative speech and action. One benefit of practice and sobriety is that they offer us a moment of peace or rest in which we can pause and decide whether to say or do something rather than just behaving impulsively. We can decide what to say in conversation rather than blurting out the first thing that comes to mind. The Vaca Sutta offers five questions we can ask about something we wish to say:

- Is it spoken at the right time and place?
- Is it spoken in truth?
- Is it spoken with affection?
- Is it spoken beneficially?
- Is it spoken with the mind of goodwill?

Perhaps a benefit of this investigation is that by the time we ask ourselves these questions, it's too late to say anything at all.

This doesn't mean that we need to avoid having difficult conversations. If our intention is to be helpful, if we are motivated by compassion or empathy or love for the person we're speaking to, we can say very difficult things to them because our intention is to cultivate greater intimacy and connection with them. If I want a deeper intimacy with a friend or partner and I have that intention in my mind and heart, then even if I am bringing up something painful or difficult, an uncomfortable truth that I need to express for my own sense of integrity, that loving intention will also be present. If we need to push ourselves toward difficult conversations by expressing anger and resentment, that anger will infect the conversation and bury our beneficial intentions.

Here are some reflections about right speech:

- Do I slander others out of jealousy, envy, or resentment?
- Do I try to build myself up by putting others down?
- Do I nurse my resentments and harbor ill will by repeating unattractive stories about other people?

Another thing we can study is the way we speak to ourselves, something that we looked at earlier. We might extend compassion to others, but even in meditation, we can be chastising ourselves for not being perfect. We may be carrying a heavy, habitual burden of negative speech about ourselves that continues to warp our experience of the world and our relationships.

When shame and guilt are topics at meetings, I remember how grateful I am for shame and guilt, because if I hadn't felt them so deeply, I might not have been motivated to change. Once we have looked honestly at our past, recovery gives us tools we can use every day to be on good terms with others and amend our speech and behavior when we need to.

We don't have to drag around our negative self-talk anymore. In studying the self, we can gently let go of automatic negativity. We can notice such thoughts and remind ourselves that we don't need to talk to ourselves that way. We can substitute a loving, wise inner friend in place of the critic. Here are some useful reflections:

- How do I talk to myself about the world?
- About myself?
- About other people?

Though I can think of things that I wish I hadn't said, there are things that I wish I had said at the appropriate time—times when I didn't have the courage to speak up in support of another, when I remained silent in the face of injustice, when I didn't counter a sexist comment. As Dr. Martin Luther King Jr. said, "In the end, we will remember not the words of our enemies but the silence of our friends."

Some reflections on this are:

- When is it appropriate to speak up?
- Will I regret it later if I don't speak up right now?

Another aspect of right speech is right listening. Perhaps we put too much emphasis, in this cell phone and email world, on speaking and forget about the need for deep listening. Sometimes we are so busy formulating and expressing our own opinions and topics of conversation that we lose sight of the healing power of silence—listening quietly to another person with an open heart and mind. To listen to another, without judgment or agenda, without offering an opinion or advice. For many of us, our first experience of being listened to in this way was in recovery.

There is a kind of humility in right listening, a humility in knowing that whatever we have to say just represents our necessarily limited point of view. My truth is valuable but not more or less valuable than yours.

---

## Reflections and Practices

As we train ourselves to restrain from impulsive words or deeds, we can stop and ask ourselves:

- Will this action lead to greater suffering, or will it help ease suffering for myself and others?
- Is this action beneficial to others but not to me?
- Is it beneficial to me but not to others?
- Is it beneficial to all?
- Sometimes right action means not doing anything. Is that the correct response here?

Asking ourselves about our motives and the appropriate course of action can help us refrain from doing harm. We have the newfound freedom of not responding instinctually, the way we used to, and instead considering the consequences of our behavior. When unclear about what we should do, we can postpone our response until the right way becomes clear. Before taking action, we can turn toward our spiritual friends and open ourselves to the wise counsel of others. The precepts are not a strict code of ethics, carved in stone. They are a guide for living in harmony, at peace with ourselves and others.

## Kshanti Paramita: The Perfection of Patience

To transform your suffering, your heart has to be as big as the ocean.

—Thich Nhat Hanh

The Buddha offered us this teaching on patience: If you put a handful of salt in a small bowl of water, it will be too salty to drink. But if you pour it into a river, the river can accept it without harm and flow on. If we are small-minded and shut off from others, a small word can enrage us, because we are trapped in a small prison of defended self-interest. But if we can widen our hearts and think bigger, if we have compassion and understanding for the suffering of others, we aren't so easily harmed by them. We can widen our circle of patience and compassion, even for those with whom we might be in conflict. Practicing patience with the ups and downs of every day, we develop the patience to endure and learn from the more difficult and painful times of our lives, days of discouragement, loss, and sorrow.

In recovery, we learn to give others a break and to be patient with ourselves. We are on a long and winding road, and we will sometimes falter along the way. But patience, and our friends in recovery, can sustain us and help us continue. We say to one another, "Keep coming back," which also means, "Be kind to yourself, and if you slip, come back. We will be patient with you. We will love you until you can love yourself." If we tend to be restless, irritable, and discontent, we can counter that habitual way of being with intentional patience. And of course, when we can be patient with ourselves, when we are humble about our own misadventures and shortcomings, we can extend that generosity and patience to others.

The seed of impatience can escalate into anger and even violence. How often have we heard of an incident of "road rage" erupting into tragedy and loss of life?

In our hurried world, we can give one another the gift of patience.

---

## Reflections and Practices

How can we cultivate patience?

- We can walk more slowly.
- We can limit our use of cell phones so we are available to the people we are with.
- We can stop talking about how busy and stressed out we are.
- When impatience arises, we can stop and breathe deeply.
- If we are forced by circumstances to sit and wait, rather than allowing impatience to sweep through us, we can enjoy the moment and experience what there is to see, hear, and feel.
- We can pause at the beginning of the day before we rush out into the world. Setting our intention for the day, we can remind ourselves of the peace, joy, and connection that are available to us when we practice patience with ourselves and others.

- If we have a meditation practice, the posture and breathing of meditation are themselves patience.
- During the day, if we feel our patience slipping away, we always have time for three deep breaths.
- We always have time to extend our hearts out to others by silently repeating to ourselves the healing words of the Metta Sutta (The Loving-Kindness Meditation): "May all beings be happy, may they be joyous and live in safety."
- If we are stuck in traffic or waiting in line, we can embody patience by letting someone else go ahead of us.
- At the end of the day, we can review our behavior and honestly assess if we are living up to our intentions.

Be patient with all that remains unanswered in your own heart and learn to love the questions themselves.
—Rainer Maria Rilke, *Letters to a Young Poet*

## Virya Paramita: The Perfection of Wholehearted Effort

To make our effort, moment after moment, is our way.
—Suzuki Roshi

Because of our habits of mind, we can get stuck in fear and negativity and despair. In Tibetan, this is called *shenpa*, the sticky nature of our deeply habitual negative thoughts. Practicing the paramitas or perfections is a way to cross over to the other shore from our unhelpful and unskillful states of mind to a new freedom. To recover from the deeply painful habit of addiction, we need to revolutionize the way we think and behave, and the paramitas can help us do that. Whether we are in recovery or not, we can all benefit from the practice of turning from unwholesome habitual thoughts to a more positive and helpful way of being.

When Suzuki Roshi came to San Francisco from Japan, he meditated every morning at Sokoji Temple in Japantown. Slowly a group of Westerners were drawn to him and began to sit zazen or meditation with him. He was attracted to what he called the "beginner's mind" of these rather rebellious and bohemian young people. They didn't have a lot of preconceptions about Buddhism; they had a kind of energetic open-mindedness that he wanted to work with. In Shunryu Suzuki's classic *Zen Mind, Beginner's Mind*, he says, "In the beginner's mind, there are many possibilities, but in the expert's mind there are few." To cultivate this kind of flexible mind, open to possibility, ready to look clearly at things in a new way, is also important in recovery.

When he was asked, "What is wholehearted effort?" Suzuki Roshi said, "Getting up when the wake-up bell rings." He was talking about monastic life, and I had the good fortune to practice at Tassajara, Zen Center's monastery in the Los Padres National Forest east of Big Sur. Every morning at 4:30, the *shuso*, or head student, runs along the path between the cabins, ringing a bell to wake everyone up to come to the zendo, the meditation hall. It's very tempting, when you are snuggled up in your warm bed, to think, "I'll just lie here for a few more moments and enjoy the warmth. I can still be on time for meditation." But it's a very different practice to just get up when you hear the bell and wash your face, brush your teeth, put on your robes, and go to the zendo.

When my teacher, Linda, asked me to come to Green Gulch to be shuso and help her lead a practice period, I had been living in the city in an apartment with my daughter and hadn't lived in a monastic setting for a while.

I told her, "I'm always afraid that I'm going to sleep through the wake-up bell."

She smiled. "That won't be a problem. Because you will be the shuso, and the shuso *rings* the wake-up bell."

What is "wholehearted effort" in our daily lives? No one is ringing a wake-up bell to get us up and encourage us to practice. How can we manifest this effort in our practice and recovery?

The first thing we need to do to practice wholehearted effort is to take good care of ourselves. Recent studies on both brain science and happiness affirm some optimum actions that we can take to have healthy lives: spending time in nature, having strong social connections with others, getting regular exercise, practicing generosity, finding a purpose in our lives, expressing our creativity, bringing novelty into our routines, and meditating—particularly on loving-kindness. We need to take care of this body, eating wholesome food, getting enough sleep, finding physical activities that we enjoy. Without this body, we can't wake up to our lives.

We need to find like-minded people, people who want what we want, who can encourage us to be our best selves. There will always be challenging people in our lives, people who "push our buttons" or bring us down. So it's important to have spiritual friends who can help us along the path, who can encourage us to be who we want to be rather than sinking back into our negative, habitual ways of thinking and acting.

Taking care of ourselves and being with loving friends can help us have healthy minds and bodies. And I think we need a little faith, the faith that we are on the right track and moving in the right direction. I have already shared with you this wonderful quote from Dogen Zenji, words that have been central to my own practice and recovery:

> To have faith means to believe that one is already inherently in the Way; and not lost, deluded, or upside down; and no increase and no decrease and no mistake.

These words encourage me to believe that no matter how I may have failed, no matter what I have done in the past that I might be ashamed of, I can have compassion for myself and recognize that my good heart and good intentions keep me moving forward in a "good orderly direction." All my missteps were steps on the path that lies ahead and continues.

If we take care of ourselves, if we live the principles of recovery, we can cultivate the energy, the humility, and the integrity to be worthy of helping others.

The Buddha taught that we are all already enlightened—we just don't realize it. Wholehearted effort requires us to take good care of ourselves, to find and cultivate positive friendships, to have the discipline and faith to be true to our recovery. And to have faith that we are always on the path of awakening.

There is a helpful image in Buddhism of watering seeds. We can always water the negative or positive seeds within us. If we are conscious of our thoughts and feelings and impulses—and meditation and mindfulness help us to be aware of them—we can either continue to think and speak and behave in habitual negative ways, or we can learn to turn in a more positive and wholesome direction. We can water the seeds of compassion, happiness, and joy, or we can water the seeds of despair, hatred, and dissatisfaction.

We often don't recognize that we have the freedom to do this. We may think we are just stuck with whoever we are. We may unconsciously repeat the negativity that we experienced in our family of origin. Growing up, we assumed that the way our parents chose to live was "normal." There may have been violence in the home, alcoholism, mental illness, and we might have felt that the things we saw and heard and felt were normal because we had nothing to compare them to. We were like fish swimming in water who don't know what water is. But when we step onto the path of practice and recovery, we learn that we aren't condemned to repeat the family karma we have inherited.

In our monthly full moon ceremony at Zen Center, we chant, "All my ancient, twisted karma, from beginningless greed, hate, and delusion, born from body, speech, and mind, I now fully avow." If there is a long chain of suffering and addiction in our family history, we have the honor and the privilege to break that chain with our recovery and the recovery we can inspire in others.

So much of what we do in recovery is an effort to reimagine our lives, to recognize that we aren't enslaved by what we've done in the past. With a beginner's mind, we can learn new ways of being in the world. Central to this is the realization that we have something to offer. If we have one day of recovery, we have something to offer someone else.

It takes a great deal of wholehearted effort to learn and practice new habits and routines. We do this through diligently working our recovery program, whatever that might be, by learning how to be honest with ourselves and others, by doing service, by stacking chairs at the end of the meeting, by reaching out to others. Rather than living in the stagnant pool of self that is addiction, we turn our will and our lives over to a new way of life, a way of life that requires rigorous honesty and wholehearted effort.

Sometimes, I don't want to go to a meeting, but my sobriety wants to go. My sobriety stands up, grabs my car keys, and takes me to the meeting place. And I go there because there were other people there for me when I needed to get sober. I want to be there for others.

In recovery, we learn to say yes. In practice, we learn to say yes. This is the enactment of wholehearted effort.

> When you say "Yes" you forget all about yourself and are refreshed into some new self. Before the new self becomes the old self, you should say another "Yes!"
> —Suzuki Roshi

We can water the seeds of ease and joy within us and, in practice and recovery, we can be with people who help us do this. When habitual negativity arises, we can notice it, turn toward gentleness and tenderness, and choose to replace that negativity with a new way of being. This takes wholehearted effort. We come to know that wholehearted effort feels good, that "in effort, there is joy." When I find myself spiraling down into negativity, I can have the presence of mind to take a deep breath and recite part of the Loving-Kindness Sutra:

> May all beings be happy,
> May they be joyous and live in safety.

And I can go to a meeting and extend my recovery to others.

*Reflections and Practices*

Write about these in your journal or share them with a trusted friend:

- Go back to your childhood and remember a time when you experienced the truth that "in effort there is joy." Was it learning to ride a bike, mastering your multiplication tables, creating a handmade gift and offering it to someone you loved?
- Think about the mistakes you had to make on the way to mastering a new skill. What does wholehearted effort look like as you walk the path of recovery? We've had to make new friends and let go of old ideas. How have you been able to do this?
- We make an effort all day, every day. Think about and give yourself credit for all the ways that your wholehearted effort benefits others—your family, your work, your sangha, your recovery.

## Dhyana and Prajna Paramitas: The Perfections of Meditation and Wisdom

Meditation practice helps us relinquish old, painful habits; it challenges our assumptions about whether or not we deserve happiness. It also ignites a very potent energy in us. With a strong foundation in how to practice meditation, we can begin to live in a way that enables us to respect ourselves, to be calm rather than anxious, and to offer caring attention to others instead of being held back by notions of separation.

—Sharon Salzberg, *Tricycle Magazine*, Spring 2011

As we practice with the paramitas and rely on them to help us recover, we have the ability, in every moment, to cross over to the shore of joy and ease. The Buddha offered his teachings as a kind of medicine, and in a way, each of the paramitas is an antidote to very human habits that cause suffering to ourselves and others. Generosity is an antidote to self-centered fear. Patience is an antidote to anger and hatred. Ethical behavior is an antidote to delusion. Wholehearted effort is an antidote to inertia and hopelessness.

Now, we come to the final paramitas—meditation (dhyana) and wisdom (prajna). These principles are antidotes to isolation and ignorance. They are inseparable from one another, but then, all the paramitas reflect back and rest on one another.

Meditation has been described as a state of mind that doesn't grasp or reject anything. There are two aspects to meditation: *shamatha* and *vipassana*.

*Shamatha* might be translated from the Sanskrit as "tranquility of mind" or "mind calming." As people in recovery, we can remember the insatiability of the addicted mind, a state of being that is constantly dissatisfied, running here and there, seeking comfort and happiness, caught up in all kinds of old ideas. In our addiction, we thrashed around, stuck in the past or living in fantasies about the future, never at rest. In practicing shamatha, we engage in mindful breathing, mindful walking, mindful sitting. We put out the fires that rage in the mind, body, and emotions. We stay put in the present moment.

*Vipassana* refers to the practice of looking deeply into the nature of things. Slowing down and paying attention, we know that everything is in a state of flux, changing moment after moment, even ourselves.

In Zen, we practice shikantaza, or just sitting. This practice was described at the beginning of this book, and it is simplicity itself—sitting cross-legged on a cushion or upright in a chair, being present for each moment. Fully awake and aware in our mind/body, we enact our vow to live an awakened life.

Most of us have found that, in order to recover, we need one another. It is deeply encouraging to our practice to find kindred spirits who want what we want, who want to cross from the shore of suffering and limitation to find a new way of being in the world.

At the same time, there is a world of suffering that cries out for our compassion and our help. One thing that can happen in the stillness of meditation is that something arises in us, an inmost desire, and we recognize that there is someplace in the world where we can lend comfort and help. We sit down to meditate, and we get up with the intention of being of use in the world.

If we try to take on the burden of the entire suffering world, we will always feel overwhelmed, inadequate to the task. Find a place where you can be useful, where you can contribute your passion and energy, and do that thing completely.

For me, that place was my third-grade classroom. I taught my students about Mexico, about Bay Area ecosystems, and about the Indigenous people of California. We learned about trees; we read books, made models, and learned how to use math in our everyday lives. But my students taught me a lot too. I remember uttering the cliché, "Great minds think alike." Paul frowned and raised his hand. "No, they don't!" he said. "That's what makes them great!" My students were luminous beings arriving at the door of my classroom to teach me generosity, patience, whole-hearted effort, ethical behavior, meditation, and wisdom every day.

When we meditate, it doesn't look like we're doing much. We don't sit to become spiritual heroes. We sit to settle into who we are, to become intimate with ourselves. We have this very rare opportunity, in our stressed-out and sped-up culture, to just *be*. And to do this in the company of others is especially encouraging and healing.

When we practiced with the mindfulness bell in my class-room, I would tell my students, "All day long, your teachers are asking you to do things, to think about things, to make things, to practice things. When you hear the mindfulness bell, stop what you are doing, take three deep breaths, and have a few moments to just *be*, without having to accomplish anything or be anyone special."

All five of the perfections, or paramitas, are included in the final one, Prajna Paramita—wisdom beyond wisdom.

In recovery, it is a common practice to ask for the serenity to accept the things we cannot change, the courage to change the things we can, and the wisdom to know the difference. This intention reminds us that we can't change other people, that there are things in the world that need changing that I won't be able to change, that I can't always get what I want, nor should I.

But we *can* change our own habitual thoughts and actions. We can learn to offer generosity and patience to ourselves and oth-ers, we can learn to live with integrity, we can exert wholehearted effort. We can make room in our lives for times of quiet reflection and meditation so we can transform our presence in the world. In terms of the paramitas, this is the wisdom to know that I can, in this moment, cross from the shore of limitation and addiction to the shore of acceptance, forgiveness, joy, and ease.

But there is a very useful term I've come across in my studies, something called "spiritual bypassing." This is something that can happen in spiritual communities where, rather than working with and understanding conflict, rather than looking deeply and practicing thoughtfully with our own strong emotions, we pretend that we're all spiritual and everything's just fine, thank you very much. We feel that we're way too evolved to feel resentful or selfish or angry, and we can drive these very human feelings underground where they continue to push us around.

In recovery, we learn about some very helpful tools to help us clean out and heal our wounds rather than slapping Band-Aids over them. Because we don't want to repeat the past, we work with it, study it, learn from it. When we look deeply at our own greed, hatred, and ignorance through the practice of recovery, prajna/wisdom/our original mind is available to us. When we learn to be generous, to find patience within ourselves, when we behave ethically and exert wholehearted effort, it's as though we are putting down a heavy burden.

In recovery, we call this burden the bondage of self. In Zen, Dogen counsels us to "settle the self on the Self," to settle our small, selfish, self-interested, grasping, ignorant self on a larger ground of being. We might call this larger Self our "higher power." In meditation, we connect with something unconditional—a state of mind that doesn't grasp at or reject anything. When we engage in shikantaza, things are allowed to come and go. We connect with a kind of unconditional openness, and that's why we can feel refreshed and renewed by it. We rest gently in the present moment rather than clinging to thoughts and feelings or pushing them away. Of course, thoughts and feelings arise when we sit. They fade into the background as we return again and again to the touchstone of the present moment. This returning is, itself, practice.

When we begin to recover from our addictions—whether to substances, behaviors, or negative and limiting habits of mind—we can also feel a kind of nostalgia for our old ways of being. When we cultivate generosity, we remember that it can feel comforting to hold on tightly. When we cultivate patience, we might feel nostalgia for our wild, uninhibited emotions, our mad adventures, our passionate anger and comfortable self-centeredness.

Part of recovery is allowing space to mourn the loss of our old habits and behaviors, and our drinking and using buddies, because it's clear that for a time we got some kind of comfort or release from them. We have to thoroughly recognize and honor that—and have compassion for the addict in ourselves. At the same time, we recognize that, in recovery, worlds we never knew existed are available to us.

We always remember that we walk this path of recovery and awakening, not just for ourselves, but because the world needs compassionate, awakened people. We offer our recovery and our practice to all beings in the ten directions, past, present, and future, and to the health and welfare of the planet. We awaken our generosity, discipline, patience, and effort; we open to meditation and wisdom. And in doing so, we become more fully ourselves.

## Reflections and Practices

- In recovery, we tap into the wisdom of those who have forged the path of sobriety ahead of us. Most of us have proven beyond a shadow of a doubt that we couldn't get sober all by ourselves. Think of someone who has been particularly helpful to you in recovery and write them a letter of gratitude.

- In our Zen practice, we bow to our cushion to acknowledge the centuries of practitioners who precede us. Think of someone who has been instrumental in opening the Way for you. It could be a teacher; it could be someone who gave you a book long ago. It could be someone who, through their own example, attracted you to practice as a precious way of life. Write them a letter of gratitude.

- Sitting quietly in your zazen posture, bring to mind as many beings as you can, throughout your life, who helped you become who you are. Your first-grade teacher, a parent or grandparent, trusted friends, a shaggy dog who loved you, those in your recovery fellowship, and those in your Buddhist sangha. There are so many! As their faces float before you, silently offer them your deepest thanks.

# 13

## The Serenity Prayer

God, grant me the serenity to accept the things I cannot
    change,
The courage to change the things I can,
And the wisdom to know the difference.
       —Adapted from a prayer by Reinhold Niebuhr

IN THE YEAR 2001, I began to lead retreats for people in recovery at the San Francisco Zen Center's Green Gulch Farm. Soon we were a group of Zen practitioners in recovery, coleading a Monday evening gathering in the Buddha Hall in the city to share how Buddhist teachings and the principles of recovery can help overcome addictions to substances and self-defeating behaviors. While all of us recognize and treasure the beauty and dynamism of Zen practice, we continue in our recovery programs, knowing that, without sobriety as a priority, there could be no true practice.

It is difficult, if not impossible, for someone to take up the Buddha Way if they are still caught up in the debilitating distractions of addictive behavior. At the heart of any recovery program is the simple but profound transformative power of one person helping another. This is a vivid enactment of the bodhisattva path, the Bodhisattva Vow to live for the benefit of all beings. To hear the cries of the world, to open our hearts to one another.

The author Andres Dubus II stopped one night to help some disabled motorists who were stranded on the side of the road. An oncoming car swerved, killing one of the people that Dubus was helping. Dubus was able to push the other person out of the way, but the car hit him, crushing his legs and leading to life in a wheelchair.

In an interview, Dubus was asked, "Do you ever ask, why me?"

Dubus replied, "That's not a helpful question. Everyone gets hit by something in this life. Everyone gets hit by some dark thing that comes rolling down the road when you don't expect it and knocks a hole in the middle of your life."

In this broad sense, we're all recovering from something—an illness, an unexpected loss, the end of a relationship, the death of a loved one or a cherished hope. As Hamlet put it, "The thousand natural shocks that flesh is heir to."

Many of us come to Buddhist practice after a life-changing event. Something that comes down the road and knocks a hole in the middle of our lives. In the midst of suffering, we have an insight that there might be another way to live. The dark thing that knocked a hole in my life was acting out my addiction despite continued negative consequences.

The Serenity Prayer is central to many recovery groups. In this prayer, we ask to be granted "the serenity to accept the things we cannot change, the courage to change the things we can, and the wisdom to know the difference." The prayer is attributed to Reinhold Niebuhr, a twentieth-century American theologian, who wrote it around 1932, and it has been adapted and adopted by many recovery programs. Niebuhr was a leading public intellectual and commentator and won the Presidential Medal of Freedom in 1964.

I have found the Serenity Prayer to be perfectly congruent with Buddhist practice. In these words, serenity is aligned with being able to accept things over which we have no control, yet at the same time having the courage—the word *courage* comes from the French word for "heart"—having the heart to take action and change what should be changed. Changing our behavior in positive ways, working toward peace and justice, being of service in a troubled world. In living this way, wisdom opens to us.

We find a similar theme in the words of Shantideva, an eighth-century Indian Buddhist monk. In Pema Chödrön's book *No Time to Lose: A Timely Guide to the Way of the Bodhisattva*, Shantideva says,

> If there's a remedy when trouble strikes,
> What reason is there for despondency?
> And if there is no help for it,
> What use is there in being sad?

One thing we can't control, much as we might like to, is other people. Much of our suffering comes from wanting things to be different than they are, especially wanting the people in our lives to be different and more in line with our needs and expectations.

From Shantideva, we learn,

> If those who are like wanton children
> Are by nature prone to injure others,

What point is there in being angry?
Like resenting fire for its heat?

And if their faults are fleeting and contingent,
If living beings are by their nature wholesome,
It's likewise senseless to resent them—
As well be angry at the sky for having clouds.

Shantideva points to our own anger, our own resentment and dissatisfaction as a means to wake up:

The cause of happiness comes rarely,
And many are the seeds of suffering,
But if I have no pain, I'll never long for freedom.
Therefore, o my mind, be steadfast!

If we expect others to be different, if we expect them to conform to some idea we have, if we expect life to be different, we will always be easily provoked. But as we practice, sitting quietly, following our breath, noticing that feelings come and go like clouds, the mind can become less reactive, more flexible, more resilient. The same situations that used to cause us suffering may no longer trouble us. At the same time, if we don't confront our own pain, we may not be motivated to change the things we can.

We can cultivate the courage to change our attitude, to develop the resilience to meet our lives face-to-face, to wake up. Shantideva says,

To cover all the earth with sheets of hide—
Where could such amounts of skin be found?

But simply wrap some leather round your feet,
And it's as if the whole earth had been covered!

If we have the courage and ability to change something that should be changed, we can do that. But if we have no control over causes and conditions, why let it disturb our equanimity?

When he was diagnosed with lung cancer in 1995, my father, Terry Burges, put his affairs in order, closed his office, and tied up any loose ends that could have distracted him from a graceful exit from this life. He didn't have a program of recovery, but he lived the Serenity Prayer, though he didn't call it that. The serenity to accept that he was terminally ill and, along with that, each new level of disability; the courage to face cancer and fight as hard as he could to maintain his quality of life and enjoy something about each day that was granted to him; and the wisdom to know that, though this cancer would end his life, it didn't define his life. One thing he continued to do after he closed his business was to notarize documents for people. I would go to visit him at the Coming Home Hospice in San Francisco where he spent his last days, and he would be asleep, with a ten-dollar bill tucked in his pajama pocket. He had just notarized someone else's will.

Living a year beyond the six-month diagnosis he was given by his doctors, my father gave his children and grandchildren a great gift. He allowed my brother Peter, my sister Betsy, my daughter Nova, and me to take care of him and be with him at his most vulnerable. This was a man who had always been defiantly self-reliant; warm, friendly, and garrulous, yet very private. He often seemed to sink into a dark and distant place, sitting on the couch with a pack of Lucky Strikes and a glass of sherry at his side, where no one else could follow him. It was a courageous act of generosity for him to allow others in, to allow us to be of help to him because *we* needed to do that.

In his book *How We Die*, Sheldon Nuland says, "The dignity in any death is in the life that precedes it." My dad refused to dwell on regrets or resentments, even those that might have seemed justified. He left this life on good terms with all beings. Looking at and appreciating the scope of his life—the world travel, the love of two wives and his children and grandchildren, the camping trips, work, the small delights of everyday life—my dad said to me, though he was in pain, dreadfully shrunken in his single hospice bed, "I'm one lucky fella."

Years before, when I was practicing at Tassajara Zen Mountain Center, my dad came down to visit me during the summer, when the monastery and hot springs open for summer guests. He spent a few days in the mountain valley, swimming in the outdoor pool and enjoying the baths. When he was about to leave, I said to him, "Dad, I'm surprised you haven't asked me anything about why I'm here. Aren't you curious about Zen?"

He answered, "You know, honey, I don't have much use for philosophy or religion. When I wake up in the morning, I just think, 'Every day is a good day.'"

I said, "Well, there was this Zen master named Yunmen who said the same thing."

To allow others to help us, to refuse to regret the past, to live our lives fully, not to leave the burden of an unlived life for our children to carry: this is serenity, acceptance, courage, and wisdom. My father burnt up in a bright flame, finished with this life.

When my dad died, Arielle, one of my third graders, made me a beautiful sympathy card: "Just when you think everything is going great . . . Death! Arrgh!!!"

In recovery, we have the serenity to accept that we have a disease that wants to destroy us. We cultivate the courage to turn in a different direction and live with the equanimity of recovery. And we have the wisdom to know that, as long as we remember who we are and where we come from, as long as we align ourselves with the principles of recovery and with people who want recovery, we never have to return to those self-destructive ways of being.

After I had been sober for a while, I felt that I was traveling on parallel train tracks. The track I live on is the track of awakening and recovery, of compassion and health. Running along right next to this track is my alcoholism and my tendency toward self-destruction, always there, right next to me. As long as I live with serenity, courage, and wisdom, I never have to move over to that dark track that runs alongside me, the track that tells me my addiction isn't that bad and there is nothing wrong with having a drink with an old friend. Now and then, I look over to that other track and say, "Hello, yes, I see you there." I have been able to cultivate compassion for the young woman who staggered around Juneau, Alaska, alone in the dark and the cold. She is right here with me.

I know in my bones that there is absolutely nothing in life that will be better if I pick up a drink. And the Serenity Prayer has been a welcome companion on this path of awakening, these shining train tracks that stretch out before and behind me forever.

---

## Reflections and Practices

Practice with the Serenity Prayer or create your own version of it. Here are some verses that you might like to memorize and practice with when you need to renew your commitment to recovery or require a moment of encouragement and peace during the day:

May all the Buddhas and Ancestors
who have attained the Buddha Way
be compassionate to us
and free us from karmic effects,
allowing us to practice the Way
without hindrance.

—Dogen Zenji

Our higher power is as close as our breath.
Conscious awareness of its presence
strengthens us moment by moment.
The past is gone;
today is full of possibilities.
With each breath,
I will be aware of the strength at hand.

—Karen Casey,
*Each Day a New Beginning*

Rest in natural great peace this exhausted mind,
beaten helpless by karma and neurotic thoughts,
like the relentless fury of the pounding waves
in the infinite ocean of samsara.
Rest in great natural peace.

—Nyoshul Khen Rinpoche

Breathing in, I know that I am breathing in.
Breathing out, I know that I am breathing out.
Breathing in, I dwell in the present moment.
Breathing out, I know this is a wonderful moment.

—Thich Nhat Hanh

At your home altar, after you sit, you can chant the Metta
Sutta, the Teaching on Loving-Kindness, or the Homage
to the Perfection of Wisdom, which you will find in the
back of this book.

# 14

## Erroneous Imaginations

When erroneous imaginations cease, the acquiescent mind realizes itself.

—Tozan Ryokai, "Hokyo Zanmai"
("Song of the Jewel Mirror Samadhi")

AT ZEN CENTER, we chant the "Hokyo Zanmai," or "Song of the Jewel Mirror Samadhi," and it tells us that when erroneous imaginations cease, the acquiescent mind realizes itself. When we loosen the grip of our self-created suffering, our flowing, flexible, Big Mind is able to shine forth.

Perhaps our most pervasive erroneous imagination is, "I am alone, a stranded individual in my own tiny boat." Actually, we are deeply connected to all things and all beings. The air we breathe is given to us by the trees; the ground supports us; without the sun, we couldn't exist for a single moment. Each person we encounter becomes part of our mind/body through the five senses that literally bring them inside us. Perhaps we would treat one another differently and would feel more at home in the world if we kept in mind the Buddha's notion that each person we meet was our mother in another lifetime.

An erroneous imagination that I entertained for years was the idea that I could drink like other people. I did drink like other people, but those other people were alcoholics. This erroneous imagination, this idea that somehow, someday, I could learn to control and enjoy drinking, took me to dark and dangerous places. Until I awakened to the truth that even one drink is too many—and that a thousand aren't enough—I was powerless over alcohol and its consequences.

There is an ancient curse, often attributed to the Chinese but more likely originating from England: "May you live in interesting times." We are living in interesting times. Navigating a global pandemic, witnessing the ravages of climate change, surrounded by rampant Orwellian doublespeak, looking askance at the deep divisions and rancor in our communities. Around the world there are mass migrations, ongoing wars, shortages of clean water and air, people living in terrible poverty. A startling example of our interconnection with one another is the way in which a pandemic can travel quickly around the world from being to being. This is a time of not knowing what is going to happen next, and this kind of uncertainty can draw us into a constant state of unease. Our imagination can lead us to fearful places. As I heard someone in a meeting say, "My mind is a dangerous neighborhood."

Fear is often an erroneous imagination. When we fear the future, our imagination can run away with us, conjuring up every possible worst-case scenario. We can also fear the past in the form of regret, thinking that we can never undo the harm we have done, that we have warped our lives. We fear that we have created problems in the past that we can't begin to unravel. We create a whole reality about the future or past and then forget that we made it all up. We can forget to notice that not all the disasters we imagine come to pass. A tremendous amount of our energy and awareness can go into these kinds of imaginings. When we are trapped in this fearful state of mind, we don't notice that we have abandoned the present moment.

We can have the same response to both imagined danger and real danger. Physiologically, we shut down when we are in fear; our vision becomes narrow, our breath quick, our palms sweaty, our choices limited. Our awareness becomes similar to looking through the wrong end of a telescope, and we no longer have the full range of our consciousness at our disposal. Distracted by fear, we are no longer here. This morass tends to lessen the time, ability, and energy we might have turned toward doing something to help the world and other people.

I've heard people in recovery characterize fear as "False Evidence Appearing Real," another way of citing erroneous imaginations. Now we can step back a bit and watch fear arise, just as we watch our breath. We can say, "Oh, there you are, my old friend fear." We can look down and see our feet on the ground, look around at the world that surrounds us, and say to ourselves, "Right now, I'm okay." Practice enables us to cultivate an open, flexible, responsive mind, the acquiescent mind of the "Hokyo Zanmai."

In the grip of fear, I can open to it, breathe into it, stay with it. We may feel guilt or shame about "negative" emotions such as fear and anger, but this just adds suffering to suffering. These emotions aren't always negative. Fear can be an important protection from real dangers; anger can spur us to action against injustice.

Dogen says, "Settle the self on the Self." We can settle our small, frightened self on Big Mind, a deeper ground of being that we sometimes glimpse in meditation or at unexpected moments in our lives.

Here is a list of the five fears in Buddhist teachings:

- Fear of loss of livelihood
- Fear of loss of reputation
- Fear of loss of life
- Fear of unusual states of mind
- Fear of speaking in front of an assembly

And, of course, fear of being stuck somewhere with nothing to read.

Most people have probably been prey to these fears at times. They are particularly vivid for those of us in recovery, because our livelihood, our reputation, our very lives were threatened by the rash and self-destructive actions we took when under the influence. Many of us spent years seeking unusual states of mind because we weren't comfortable with the ones we already had. We speak of having needed to take a drink, or a few, before a social event so we would have the courage to talk to other people. When I was drinking, I lived constantly with a feeling of impending doom. Looking back, I know now what that feeling was. It was impending doom. Fear is a gift if it motivates us to seek sobriety.

One of the first Zen stories I heard was a story the Buddha told of a man who is running across a field being chased by a tiger. Holding on to a vine, he swings himself over the edge of a cliff and sees another tiger down below, licking its chops and waiting for him. Just then, a white mouse and a black mouse crawl out of a hole and start nibbling on the vine. He looks over and sees a strawberry growing close by. He grasps it—and how sweet it tastes! This is a metaphor for life—fearful, tenuous, fraught with difficulty and suffering, ultimately fatal, and . . . also sweet.

An antidote to erroneous imaginations, an antidote to paralyzing fear, is to remember the preciousness of having been born a human being and to understand impermanence.

## Appreciating the Preciousness of Human Life

It is easy to appreciate our human lives if we narrowly escape some accident or survive some traumatic event along with other people. In recovery, we find other people who have faced and survived a life-threatening disease, and we share a joyful relief and camaraderie that we don't necessarily find anywhere else.

When we collectively go through a frightening episode, it can bring out the inherent heroism and generosity of human beings. People seem a little kinder, a little more gracious than usual. Letting others into traffic, talking to strangers. We slow down a bit because we experience more deeply the preciousness and revocability of human life.

Through Buddhism, we realize that it is a great privilege to be born as a human being. We say, "This chance rarely occurs in any lifetime," the chance to practice the Way. To be born into a human body—rather than, say, a piece of moss on a rock—is a privilege that we shouldn't squander or take for granted.

Hakuin Zenji (1686–1769), our great Zen ancestor, said, "Having had the good fortune not only to have been born into this world as a human being, but also to have encountered the teachings of the great Shakyamuni Buddha, how can we help but be overjoyed?"

During the everyday chores of life or in times of sickness or hardship, we can slip into negativity or self-pity and forget that we have these problems because they go along with being a human being in a human body. If we were a piece of moss on a rock, we wouldn't have to take out the garbage or pay taxes, we wouldn't be subject to fear or anger, resentment or envy—but, as far as I know, we also wouldn't be able to enjoy a sunset or fall in love.

Mindfulness awakens us to each moment, taking care of each thing as it arises, washing a dish with the same care we would wash a baby, tearing lettuce for the salad as tenderly as we would touch a flower. If we approach our everyday activities in this way, we awaken to the unique beauty of each moment and remember how precious it is just to be born as human beings. We can give ourselves a break from worry if we come back to the present moment and savor it.

Recovery grants us the clarity and subtlety to be available for everyday life and to take joy in simple pleasures. Rather than seeking extremity and taking risks, we can enjoy ordinary activities and find satisfaction with what is right in front of us. We can also marshal our talents, intelligence, and abilities to serve the world.

## Understanding Impermanence

One of our erroneous imaginations is mistaking the impermanent for the permanent. Zazen is literally practice for understanding impermanence. As I watch my breath come and go and watch feelings and thoughts come and go, I can see that even a difficult emotion like fear is not solid or never-ending. Each moment arises and passes away, as do all things. If I can surrender to this moment rather than living always in the past or future, I can be more fully alive and more fully myself. We want to be present for this moment because this is it—this is life itself.

This is easy to believe, easy to say, not always easy to do.

Zazen can jog us out of old ways of being, old ways of thinking, old behaviors that don't serve us today. If we practice regularly sitting down and following our breath and watching what arises, we are more likely to carry that practice into our everyday. We are more likely to notice when we are in the grip of erroneous imaginations. Zazen helps us cultivate what Suzuki Roshi called "beginner's mind," open to many possibilities. I can draw a wider circle of compassion that includes myself and others rather than being trapped in a narrow, selfish state of fear or hatred.

If we live in fear today, that will affect our future too, because we are literally missing out on our lives and the possibilities and potentialities that await us. In a real way, our actions today can affect even our past, because one way to make positive use of our remorse is to put our own preoccupations aside and help others. We find that the things we did that we were ashamed of, when shared with another, can help them identify with our story and recognize that recovery is possible, even for the most damaged and destitute.

In recovery, our fear of economic insecurity is healed by becoming more employable, by taking better care of our finances, by avoiding unnecessary spending, by paying parking tickets when they happen, by saving for the future.

Our fear of people begins to dissipate when we take responsibility for ourselves, when we tell our story, engage in service, and work with others. In recovery, I learn to "live and let live" as I sit with a diverse group of people I might never have known otherwise. I don't get up and leave a meeting because someone says something I don't like. I get there a little early, and I stay after to offer fellowship to others. I "stay"— stay in the meeting, stay with my feelings, stay with my fear and discomfort—knowing they will dissipate, as will any craving that might take hold of me.

---

## Reflections and Practices

- Sit quietly in your zazen posture for a few minutes, coming back to your breath.

When fear arises, we can reflect on these questions:

- Is this a reasonable fear, one I should listen to? When acting out in my disease, my judgment was impaired, and I was vulnerable to dangerous situations. With the clarity of sobriety, I am better able to assess a situation and respond appropriately.
- Is my imagination working overtime, conjuring up dreadful possibilities that may never come to pass?
- Am I too hungry, angry, lonely, or tired, and is this affecting my thinking?
- Am I telling myself things that aren't true? "No one cares about me. I have ruined my life forever. Nothing good will ever happen for me . . ."
- Am I projecting myself into a future problem that may never happen?

- Is the fear I'm holding on to now actually some learned fear from the past that I am ready to discard? Am I applying an old fear to a completely new situation?
- If I am afraid of financial insecurity, are there steps I can take in the present that may help my future situation?

If you find yourself spiraling into fear, anxiety, or negativity, you might bring to mind the phrase from the "Hokyo Zanmai": When erroneous imaginations cease, the acquiescent mind realizes itself.

# 15

## The Importance of Humor

I don't remember having a spiritual experience but something
sure as hell must have happened.

—Written on a blackboard at a rehab facility

EACH MORNING at the three temples associated with the San
Francisco Zen Center—City Center, Green Gulch Farm, and Tas-
sajara Zen Mountain Center—we chant the names of our ances-
tors, the men and women practitioners of our lineage who stretch
all the way back to the Buddha's time.

Tendo Nyojo (1163–1228) is an important name in this lineage,
as he gave Dharma transmission to our great ancestor Dogen
Zenji, who brought Zen from China to Japan. There is a custom
for Zen masters to spontaneously offer a poem at the time of their
death, and this was Tendo Nyojo's:

I've given you my all,
Tossing it your way with a hearty laugh.

I entrust it all to the Spring Wind,
For there is nothing more that I need to do.

"I've given you my all." Despite the truth of impermanence, of the illusory nature of this existence, still, "I've given you my all," confident that his life was complete, as if drawing a sumi circle in the air. "Tossing it your way with a hearty laugh."

In recovery, I've heard it said, "We are not a glum lot." One of the surprising things about the rooms of recovery is the laughter, which stems from the joy we feel at having survived a potentially deadly disease and living to tell the tale with our fellow survivors. Humor is important in our Zen practice as well. Suzuki Roshi endured many tragedies in his life, and though he died before I came to Zen Center, the stories I've heard about him from his students reveal both his fierceness and his buoyant sense of humor. How can we laugh when there is so much suffering in the world? Yet we have the filmed images of Suzuki Roshi, playing with a yo-yo and laughing gleefully. Perhaps this is one of the paradoxes of Zen: a Zen master of the twentieth century who has experienced great tragedy playing with a yo-yo; a Zen master of the thirteenth century tossing off his death poem with a hearty laugh.

My hope is that, for you, practice and recovery are attended by laughter. Laughter erupts from empathy, from recognition of our common plight, from seemingly disparate things coming together in surprising ways. It comes as a relief from the stresses and vagaries of life. On my bookshelf, the cartoonist Roz Chast is right next to Zen Master Dogen.

Recently, I attended an event at the Marsh Theater in San Francisco, featuring Josh Kornbluth, a local monologuist and humorist. Josh was a guest artist at the Zen Hospice Project and then a fellow at the Memory and Aging Clinic at the University of California Medical Center, where they are studying prefrontal dementia.

One of the symptoms of this form of dementia is that a previously compassionate person loses their sense of empathy and their interest in caring for others. When studied with magnetic resonance imaging (MRI), the empathy center of their brains in the prefrontal cortex is literally dark. Josh gives the example of a grandmother, previously loving and engaged with her grandchildren, suddenly expressing no warmth or interest in them, staring blankly at a baby when it is held out to her.

When Josh was a child, his father, who was a communist, told his young son that he was going to grow up to lead a communist revolution in this country. Apparently, that hasn't happened yet. But Josh has chosen for his project as guest artist at the clinic to lead a worldwide revolution in empathy. No pressure, right?

Josh asked one of the neurologists at the clinic what we can do to deepen our empathy with one another, especially at a time when there are such huge divisions and disparities in our country. He was told that if a person who has had a deep prejudice against someone, say, of another religion, has a transformative experience with a person of that other faith or race, they can begin to feel a spark of empathy within themselves. We've heard stories of former gang members or white nationalists who have been transformed by the power of love, disavowing violence and hatred.

The neurologist gave another example: storytelling. We transform one another by listening to one another's stories. When I hear your story, my brain is literally changed. The neurons in my brain include you, they make a path for you in my brain. As you speak, your image is literally in my eyes, and your voice is in my ears. When you hear my story, you are changed.

When we listen to one another with open hearts and minds, we are transformed.

This was good news for Josh, since he's a professional story-teller. Somehow he manages, in the improvs he does about his work at the clinic, to share the pathos and tragedy of these folks with great kindness, to extol the virtue of their volunteering to have their damaged brains studied, while also bringing out the humor that is there.

This is an invitation for all of us to listen to one another's stories with open hearts and minds and help a little bit with this worldwide revolution of empathy. I love stories from every tradition. Here is one I heard early in my Zen practice that has stayed with me.

Two monks were walking in the woods and came to a stream. A young woman was standing there barefoot, holding her kimono up a bit so it wouldn't get wet, unsure of how to get across.

One of the monks offered to carry her to the other side. She awkwardly climbed onto his back, piggyback style, and the three of them waded across together. The monk put her down on the other side of the stream, and the two monks went on their way, leaving the woman to make her way in the other direction.

After they had been walking in silence for a while, one of the monks spoke up.

"I can't believe that you broke your vow and carried that woman on your back!"

The other monk said, "I put her down an hour ago, but you have carried her on *your* back ever since."

It seems we begin to lose our sense of humor as we enter our twenties. According to the behavioral scientist Jennifer Aaker of Stanford University, a Gallup poll conducted in 166 countries found that the average four-year-old laughs about three hundred times a day, but it takes two and half years for a forty-year-old to accrue that much laughter. Yet, laughter has many benefits. Having a sense of humor, being able to laugh at ourselves and the vicissitudes of life can be a buffer against spiraling down into a pit of depression and dismay about the state of the world. As the American Zen master Mel Brooks says, "Humor has been my delicious refuge from the world."

Even the queen of England had her rough days. I remember several years ago part of one of her palaces burned down, and her grown children were misbehaving and being described unbecomingly in the press. In her annual New Year's speech to the nation, she said, with characteristic British understatement, "It is not a year upon which I will look back with undiluted joy."

Suzuki Roshi was a powerful presence, though only about 4 feet, 11 inches tall. In his lectures, he laughed a lot. I heard that at the beginning of a sesshin, or seven-day sitting, he said, "The problems you are having now . . . are the problems you will have for the rest of your life!" and threw back his head and laughed. Dogen Zenji might have had a pretty good sense of humor too. He referred to life as "one continuous mistake."

Here are some aspects of cultivating a sense of humor.


### Everything is always changing, so why not laugh?

One of the invitations to lighten up and have a sense of humor is that everything is constantly shifting and changing. Whatever we are upset about today may change completely tomorrow. David Chadwick, a Zen priest at Zen Center for many years and the author of Suzuki Roshi's biography, *Crooked Cucumber*, asked Roshi, "If you could sum up the truth of Buddhism in one phrase, what would it be?" And Suzuki Roshi answered without hesitation, "Everything changes."

I would have to add, except Jennifer Aniston.

### *Sometimes things are so outrageously bad that all we can do is laugh.*

Even when we are going through the darkest of times, we can find comfort in laughter with those we trust the most. For the Day of the Dead, I would ask my third graders to share a story about a pet who had died, since most of them had experienced that example of impermanence.

Kris described a time when she had gone to a soccer game, leaving her hamster to play in her room, where he liked to roam free and climb on her bunk bed.

"When I came back from my game," she said, "all of my pets were dead!" Apparently, the hamster had climbed up on the top bunk and had jumped or fallen off into the fishbowl below. The hamster drowned in the fishbowl, and all the fish were lying dead on the floor.

For a moment, there was a somber silence in the circle of kids sitting on the floor. Then one of them began to laugh, and then another, until even Kris was laughing with us. I could tell that some of the kids felt kind of bad about laughing, so I said, "It's okay, sometimes things are so bad, all you can do is laugh."

Had they been older, I might have shared Samuel Beckett's observation, "When you're up to your neck in shit, there's nothing left to do but to sing."

*Humor conveys our affection for and
connection with one another.*

Sometimes you meet someone, and you immediately know
from their sense of humor that there is an affinity there. With
old friends, we remember stories from the past that make us
laugh.

My daughter Nova and I have been through a lot together, and
we thoroughly enjoy one another's company as adults. I recently
came across a Mother's Day card she gave me a couple of years
ago. On the front it said, "I got born, I grew up, I left home, I got
a job, I'm not in prison . . ." And on the inside, "What more could
a mother want?"


*Humor can transform an argument and help you and
someone you love remember shared bonds.*

Sometimes we have a moment when we notice that we have a
choice. We can be righteously indignant, we can get puffed up
and angry, or we can find something in the situation to laugh at
or a shared memory that can melt all animosity. In my work with
children, I could get irritable, or I could make a joke. One of my
students would poke me with a finger to get my attention, and I
would say, "That's pet peeve number 1,427!"

I treasure many funny moments I shared with my third grad-
ers. I was out in Point Reyes a while ago, and I saw a former stu-
dent of mine who was then about twenty-five years old. Anna
walked up to me and shyly said, "I don't know if you remember
me, but I was in your class."

And I said, "Anna, not only do I remember you, I remember

when you raised your hand in class and said, 'Laura, what happens after you die? I forget!'"

### Humor can point to a larger truth.

I used to remind myself now and then not to be surprised when third graders acted like third graders, and then I would remember that I also shouldn't be surprised when people act like people. As my friend James says, "People. They're not what they're cracked up to be."

### Humor is often based on making connections between seemingly unconnected things.

Humor takes us by surprise. One day I was walking in the hallway behind a couple of my students, and I heard Talia say to Tess, "Would you rather be buried or cremated?" And Tess replied, "I don't know. Surprise me!"

### Self-deprecating humor has its place.

We find humility when we don't take ourselves so seriously. This can help us cultivate a kind of warm detachment. Through practice we can catch ourselves being self-righteous, and we feel a little silly. I read about a woman who felt that humility is a spiritual practice, and she found herself looking around the room thinking, "I have more humility than anyone in this room." She had to laugh out loud when she caught herself thinking that.

Maybe part of humility is to have a sense of humor even about our shortcomings. We can stop expecting ourselves to be perfect. We can transform that negative voice in our head that is chastising us for our mistakes into a loving friend who will always be there for us, even when we are not at our best.

## Laughter can come when we recognize our connection to others.

We can laugh when we recognize ourselves in another person's story, when we see ourselves in another person's foibles. We might think, "Wow, I've done that same crazy thing myself!"

## Humor is subjective.

Something I might find funny could leave you cold or vice versa. Humor can connect us or offend us. Humor is not always in good taste, not always politically correct, but it may be necessary to let off some steam. Alice Roosevelt Longworth said, "If you can't think of anything nice to say about anybody, come over here and sit by me."

## Humor relieves stress.

Studies show that humor has impressive health benefits. Laughter releases endorphins and the bonding chemical oxytocin, and it reduces cortisol, the stress hormone. Shared laughter brings strangers, coworkers, intimate partners, and family members closer together, which also reduces individual stress.

*Humor gives us the freedom to be outrageous or even offensive.*

The day after President Barack Obama was elected, the headline in the *Onion* was "Black Man Gets Worst Job in America."

We can appreciate the subversive power of humor in this country with our precious freedom of speech. I remember Chris Rock saying, "George Bush was so bad that he made it impossible for a white man to get elected after him." In the United States, comedians and cartoonists have the freedom to speak truth to power without getting arrested—at least, so far.

*Humor isn't necessarily benign; in fact, it can be quite aggressive.*

A comedian who does well, says they "killed it" or "destroyed it." If they don't do well, they "died" or "bombed."

I've listened to comics talk about their craft, and many of them were painfully shy as kids or developed humor as a defense. They talk about using a sense of humor to make a depressed parent laugh or to distract a bully on the playground when they were young.

I grew up in a household where there was a lot of teasing, and I learned to give as good as I got. One of the best compliments you could get at the dinner table was if someone teased you, and you came back with a zinger. "Good comeback!" my dad would say.

Sometimes I don't look forward to seeing someone because their default position is to mock me. The literal meaning of the word *sarcasm* is "to rip the flesh," and we can use humor at someone else's expense. I've certainly teased others or said something glib that I immediately wished I could retrieve. I like the expression, "I would have bitten my tongue if my foot hadn't been in my mouth." I notice, though, that I don't tease people I don't already feel comfortable with. Still, it's worth asking when teasing is genuine affection and when it is disguised hostility.

Of course, we should practice diligently, but I hope we can bring some silliness and generosity and humor to the path of practice and recovery. When my daughter was a teenager, she walked through the living room and glanced at a bunch of Pema Chödrön's books on the coffee table—*The Wisdom of No Escape, When Things Fall Apart, The Places That Scare You, No Time to Lose*—and Nova said, "Jeez, what a drama queen." I think Pema would like that story.

Humor can help us stop taking ourselves and our opinions so seriously. This is a form of detachment, not a cold cynical detachment, not a refusal to engage with the world, but a warmhearted detachment that comes from recognizing the truth of impermanence, from understanding that the difficulties we are experiencing, the dark time we may be going through, is just another part of the path and will pass away like everything else.

Shall we remember the words of Tendo Nyojo?

I've given you my all,
Tossing it your way with a hearty laugh
I entrust it all to the Spring Wind,
For there is nothing more that I need to do.

—Tendo Nyojo

## Reflections and Practices

Sit quietly in your zazen posture for a few minutes, coming back to your breath.

It's a helpful practice to think of humor in terms of right speech:

- Am I using humor to mock and belittle?
- Am I using humor to keep people at a distance or to disguise my real feelings or who I really am?
- Do I use humor when I honestly don't even know how I really feel?
- Am I using humor to connect with others?
- Am I using humor to diffuse a tense situation?
- Am I using humor to relieve stress and make a connection?
- Am I using humor to build bonds of affection and identification?
- Is humor a reflection of joy and love and delight at this crazy reality we find ourselves in, or is it used to shame and diminish?
- How can I use humor in a wholesome way?
- Can I find humor and at the same time avoid doing harm?

# 16

## Emotional Freedom

Do not try to save the whole world or do anything
   grandiose.
Instead, create a clearing in the dense forest of your life
and wait there patiently . . .

—Martha Postlethwaite

OUR PRACTICE AND RECOVERY are offerings to the whole world. First, we get sober for ourselves, then for the people we love, then we notice as we grow stronger that we have something to offer the world. The emotional freedom that we can find in practice and recovery is at the center of this offering. Each of us has the potential to be a flickering light in the darkness, showing one another the way.

Tara Brach is an American Buddhist teacher, psychologist, and author. In her book *Radical Compassion*, she outlines a kind of prescription for greater emotional freedom. One of the first things Tara recommends is asking yourself if you are living a life that is true to yourself. She tells of a hospice caretaker who has witnessed many people, during their last days on this earth, expressing deep regret that they hadn't lived a life that was true to themselves. Wouldn't it be wonderful to learn how to be true to ourselves now rather than living with regret at the end of our lives?

Many of us carry a recovery medallion in our pocket, which we renew each year on our sobriety date. It says, "To thine own self be true," an admonition made by Polonius in Shakespeare's *Hamlet*. Take a few moments to consider what it means to you to be true to yourself:

- Is your life in alignment with your inmost desire?
- Do you live each day keeping in mind the values that you most cherish?
- Do you notice when you veer away from your vow and make an effort to return to it?

What does it mean to be true to yourself? Each of us might answer this question in a different way. Living in accordance with the principles of recovery, being fully ourselves, being kind and thoughtful toward others while maintaining our own purpose and dignity. Finding meaningful work we love. Opening our minds and hearts to the wide world. Expressing our creativity and being available to others. Cultivating wisdom and resilience. Having the clarity to follow our own hearts rather than always doing what others expect of us. When we are true to ourselves, we can also be true to our collective path of healing and freedom.

Yet every day we can fall short of our intentions and aspirations. We may blame others for our shortcomings, indulge in our addictions, find ourselves living on automatic pilot. We may have been traumatized in the past in a way that makes us feel numb and disconnected.

This very feeling of discomfort, of being ill at ease in our skin, of waking up regretting things we've done or said, is what can open the door to recovery. In order to wake up to our lives, many of us had to come face-to-face with the realization that, trapped in the downward spiral of addiction, we could not be true to ourselves.

Before we begin our recovery, many of us have had the experience of falling down, of hitting bottom, of recognizing that we needed to instigate a profound change in our lives. This has been referred to as "deflation at depth." Our recovery can be a window to practice, turning our shame and deficiencies into ways to redeem ourselves and connect with others. There is a paradox here: to be true to ourselves, we need to take actions that will help release us from self-centered fear.

Tara shares a quote from Martha Postlethwaite: "Do not try to save the whole world or do anything grandiose. Instead, create a clearing in the dense forest of your life." We can think of this dense forest as a place where Mara resides, that afflictive being who was jealous of the Buddha's vow to sit still and penetrate reality. This is our own tendency toward distraction, addictive behavior, worry, compulsive busyness, self-criticism and judgment of others, regret and shame. These distractions can obscure our intention to be open and loving, and when we get trapped by them, we can forget who we are and what we want.

Brach says, "If we go into trance when we encounter stress— rushing around, worrying, judging—we reinforce the fear-based ruts in our mind. If, instead, we become mindful in times of stress, learning to pause and to recognize and allow our experience, something different is possible. Instead of reacting from our passing wants and fears, we can respond to our circumstances from a deeper intelligence, creativity, and care. This creates new patterning, new neural pathways in the brain that correlate with true well-being and peace."

The practice that Tara offers in her book is called RAIN, and it helps us find healing, freedom, and ease in the midst of emotional pain. She credits this technique to the meditation teacher Michele McDonald, who developed it in the 1980s, and it has been adopted by many others.

RAIN stands for:

R: Recognizing our tangle of emotions and physical sensations
A: Allowing them without resistance
I: Investigating the nature of these feelings with gentle attention
N: Nurturing ourselves; calling on our deepest self for healing

Practicing with RAIN is a way to "create a clearing in the dense forest" of our lives, to turn toward the present moment and break out of the distractions that keep us separate from our true being. Calling on RAIN when we are distressed can help us break free of deeply held beliefs and patterns that no longer serve us.

Brach says, "Radical compassion is rooted in mindful, embodied presence, and it is expressed through active caring that includes all beings." She uses the metaphor of a bird with two beautiful wings—one is compassion, the other mindfulness—and with both of these wings, we can fly. In our recovery, we step out of the limiting circle of self-centeredness and share with others what we have cultivated within ourselves. Gradually, we come to see that we have something to offer, and we feel a gradual release from the obsessiveness of self-centered fear.

Recently, I felt hurt when someone with whom I am very close made an offhand, critical remark. Rather than responding in the moment, I asked for some time. I *recognized* that I was feeling angry and hurt; I felt pressure in my chest and my face was hot. Confusion swirled around inside me. I *allowed* these feelings to just be within me, understanding that this was just where I was and that I didn't have to deny these feelings, act on them, or lash out. When I *investigated* this familiar territory, I realized that I felt belittled and dismissed, not seen, not appreciated for who I am. This was a very old feeling from deep in my past. I *nurtured* myself by giving myself some time, privacy, and silence to honor my feelings, to calm down and allow myself to settle.

When I was ready, I was able to return and speak in a loving way. I was able to see and say that I had reacted from the abandoned child within me, that I had attached some old outgrown feelings to the present moment. I also said that, as an adult, it's important to me to be treated with respect and care. In reflecting on the nature and tone of their flippant comment, the other person could understand why I was upset. As each of us shared our own experience, we were able to regain a feeling of peace with one another.

Sometimes we aren't available, even to our inmost selves. We are preoccupied, shut down. We feel overwhelmed by all that we have to do and are convinced that we won't succeed. There is a feeling of numbness, detachment, or panic. Our recovery literature calls this state being "restless, irritable, and discontent." Perhaps there is no better example of this departure from being true to ourselves than the way we acted out in our disease. We knew exactly what was going to happen when we indulged in our addictions, yet we did it once again. And once again we fell into the downward spiral of shame and regret. Tara doesn't disparage feeling deficient and disconnected, because this led her to her true self and her true calling. She discovered that she had to love herself into healing. I would say that this is also true of our efforts toward recovery.

You might notice you are in trance if you just ate a whole box of cookies without thinking about it, if you can't sit still or focus, if you are in a state of fight-or-flight, if you have spent the last hour scrolling through one YouTube cat video after another. You can ask yourself, "Right now, am I present for myself, or have I abandoned myself?"

My mantra, when I tip into overwhelm is, "I have all the time I need." When I remind myself that I have all the time I need, I break out of the addiction to busyness and open to the present moment. I walk a little more slowly, smile a little more often.

When we are gripped with a strong emotion, like anger or resentment, we can still be fully present, and our presence can temper our anger and keep us from doing something or saying something we will regret later. We can open to the anger, witness it, and decide how we want to respond. If we are in conflict with someone and feel angry, we can tell them that we need a little time to cool off before we continue talking. This gives us time to reflect on what is fueling our anger, and we may uncover a deeper feeling underneath our rage. Often when we are angry, we are ignoring a feeling of being hurt or abandoned. When those vulnerable feelings are disguised as anger and we lash out, we push away the very person we wish to be close to, which increases our feeling of being hurt and abandoned. Taking time to pause and reflect on our feelings gives us the freedom of restraint. We know that we don't have to act out, that we don't have to speak harshly to others to discharge our strong emotions. When we come back to the conversation, we can share our truth from a stronger, more compassionate place that also takes the other person into consideration.

In a very practical way, we are reeducating ourselves through the tools of recovery. Addiction cuts deep grooves into our brains and our patterns of behavior. If we are going to create new pathways in the brain, we need to learn new ways of being in the world. There's an expression in recovery, "If you hang around a barbershop long enough, you are going to get a haircut." We can't craft a new way of life if we simply return to the people we used with and the places where we used, if we keep saying and doing the things we have always said and done. With the encouragement of recovery, we are no longer compelled to react instinctually to events; we can now pause and take care of ourselves. RAIN can be part of this retraining, simple steps that we can take when we are off-balance that help us refrain from acting out and return to composure.

When we were growing up, our feelings might have been inconvenient for the adults around us. We might have been taught to bury our feelings, to be ashamed of them, to deny them. We might have been told that it was selfish to have our own feelings. When we became adults ourselves, it might have been difficult to even recognize our true feelings because we had been estranged from them for so long. If we are to live true to ourselves, we need to be able to experience the full range of our emotional lives and learn how to stay in compassionate connection with others.

What would happen if we simply said yes to our complicated emotions and gave them room to breathe?

---

## Reflections and Practices

- Sit quietly in your zazen posture for a few minutes, coming back to your breath.
- The next time you find yourself in a maelstrom of emotions, stop, breathe, and apply RAIN.
- Find some time to sit quietly and notice how you feel after going through this process. Take some deep breaths and scan your body slowly from head to toe, feeling your body from the inside out.
- If you don't feel you are living true to yourself, what can you do to move more clearly in that direction?

# 17

---

# The Healing Power
# of Forgiveness

To forgive is to set a prisoner free
and discover that the prisoner was you.

—Lewis B. Smedes

FORGIVENESS IS THE PRACTICE of softening, of gently letting go of deeply held anger and resentment. Part of our recovery is to face the harm we have done to others and to make amends. If we are going to ask for forgiveness, shouldn't we be willing to forgive? And if we are to ask others to forgive us, shouldn't we also forgive ourselves?

The Buddhist precepts, which were discussed in chapter 12, are a kind of medicine that heals suffering by shining a light on body, speech, and mind. One of the ten prohibitory precepts tells us, "A disciple of the Buddha does not harbor ill will." To harbor ill will is to cling to and identify with the ways in which we feel someone has harmed us and to hold on to a one-sided and limited view of others. In recovery, we learn that we don't have to nurse our resentments in order to be true to ourselves.

For those of us in recovery, resentment and righteous indignation are dangerous because they can lead us to a drink, a drug, or a behavior that we want to turn away from. When we are trapped in obsessive thoughts about resentment and revenge, we can't be fully present for this moment. We can't see the other person fully. We can't take responsibility for our own part in things. And we can't live our own lives with ease and joy. If we just took up the practice of forgiveness, we could enact the principles of Buddhism completely.

Phan Thi Kim Phuc was nine years old on June 8, 1972, when she was photographed running naked down a dusty road in her village in South Vietnam. Kim Phuc and other villagers had been accidentally napalmed by South Vietnamese planes and were fleeing for their lives. Nick Ut received a Pulitzer Prize for this iconic photograph, which became a searing symbol of the war and, some would say, helped turn the conscience of many Americans against it. Ut took the children to a hospital in Saigon, where Kim Phuc stayed for fourteen months, receiving seventeen surgical procedures. It wasn't until she was taken to a special clinic in Germany in 1982 that she was finally able to move properly again.

In 1996, Kim Phuc spoke at the Vietnam Veterans Memorial. She talked about how we cannot change the past, but we can work together to ensure a more peaceful future. She expressed the need to meet and forgive anyone who participated in the attack on her village. A Vietnam veteran, John Plummer, who claimed to have taken part in coordinating the air strike that had injured Kim Phuc, met with her and was publicly forgiven. Later, it came to light that, though he hadn't had a role in the air strike, he felt culpable for the suffering of the Vietnamese and had been caught up in the emotion of the moment. Since then, the two have enjoyed a lifelong friendship that has come to symbolize the power of faith and forgiveness in the wake of a terrible war that deeply affected them both. Kim Phuc has said that forgiveness has freed her from hatred. She wonders, "If the little girl in that photograph can forgive, then ask yourself, can you?" Phan Thi Kim Phuc was awarded the 2019 Dresden Peace Prize for her work with UNESCO and for her tireless activism on behalf of world peace.

Restorative justice programs create alternatives to strict punishment and help engender understanding and forgiveness. For example, in Marin County, California, two high school boys—one Black, one Latino—who had been in racially charged physical altercations with one another at school, were "sentenced" to have dinner on Sunday nights with their families at alternate households during the remainder of the school year. This helped both the boys and their families overcome their resentments and prejudices as they sampled delicious foods from their family traditions and got to know one another.

Living in the realm of anger, resentment, self-pity, jealousy, fear, and envy can never give us the freedom, peace, and connection we long for. We would do well to look closely at the way we hold on to afflictive emotions that cause suffering for ourselves and others. We can't control other people, but with practice and recovery, we learn that we can radically transform our reaction to the world and find new ways of being.

The twelfth-century Buddhist sage Shantideva asked if we should cover the whole world with leather to protect our feet, or would it make more sense just to wear shoes?

- Can we change ourselves rather than expecting the world to change to suit us?
- If we are carrying around a grievance right now, like a backpack full of rocks, can we apply teachings on forgiveness to our situation?
- Can we allow ourselves to put down this burden of grievance?

Fred Luskin, PhD, is the head of the Forgiveness Project at Stanford University. His scientific research on the medical and psychological benefits of forgiveness has benefited victims on both sides of the "troubles" in Northern Ireland's civil war, as well as many others who have suffered from the paralyzing effects of long-held resentments. Through his work, he has been able to encourage people to let go of deeply held prejudices and hatreds, helping participants see their "enemies" as human beings, with hopes, dreams, feelings, grief, and sorrow just like their own.

Henry Wadsworth Longfellow said, "If we could read the secret history of our enemies, we would find in each person's life sorrow and suffering enough to disarm all hostility." In his research on forgiveness, Luskin has found that forgiveness is not about forcing ourselves to forget painful things that have happened to us. It doesn't mean that it's fine for people to mistreat us. Forgiveness doesn't have to be a rare, mystical experience. It doesn't mean that we have to reconcile with a violent or toxic abuser. It doesn't mean denying our own experience or our own feelings. It can happen in the presence of another or in the privacy of our own hearts. Forgiveness can happen in an instant, or it can take a lifetime.

We are constantly mapping our world. For a map to be effective, it can't show every detail. A map of Europe doesn't show where the trees and houses and people are. My family tree doesn't show the personalities and joys and sorrows of the people that it lists. A blueprint shows the overhead view of a home, but it doesn't show what is inside the house or tell the story of the people who will live there. A map is helpful because it focuses on a particular slice of reality—but it only gives partial information.

Our attention is like this. If we pay attention to every single detail that comes into our awareness, we will become overwhelmed, distracted, confused. We are hearing, seeing, feeling, smelling, touching simultaneously all the time, but we are also deciding what is the most important thing to pay attention to. We divide the world up to make it more manageable—like someone making a map—but we forget that we've divided it up. We divide it up into things we like, things we don't like; things that delight us and things that irritate us. Things we cling to and things we push away. People we want to be with and people we want to stay away from.

If we have a tendency toward resentment, we forget that we are assigning that emotion to events that don't necessarily have anything to do with us. Because of past experiences, we might be on guard, trying to protect ourselves from others. This can lead us to actively look for things to be resentful about without even realizing it, mapping out a world of hurt and remembered pain, like a field of land mines that are just waiting to "get" us. We can forget that we have a choice about what we pay attention to and how we respond.

Instead of focusing on the things we resent, we could choose to focus on the things we're grateful for or the things that give us pleasure. We could focus on the precious qualities of the people we spend our lives with. We could pay attention to moments in the day when we felt especially helpful or helped.

Suzuki Roshi taught his students that the most important thing we work with in practice is our attitude. This is a truth we also encounter in recovery. If we pay special attention to the things that go wrong during the day, we are ignoring the hundreds of things that go right. If we feed and nurture and tend to our resentments, we are ignoring other things. We can't be resentful and grateful at the same time.

It's easy to see that our unresolved resentments prevent us from living fully in this moment and interfere with our ability to be of service to ourselves and others. It's easy to water the seeds of a resentment: we take things too personally; we are unwilling or unable to see our own part in a conflict; we blame the offender for the way we feel; and we create a grievance story that we tell to anyone who will listen, even strangers in an elevator. You may be carrying a painful story about a past hurt. In his book *Forgive for Good: A Proven Prescription for Health and Happiness*, Dr. Luskin suggests the following:

- Allow yourself to feel this hurt right now. Let it fill your mind and body.
- Recognize that this feeling of pain is understandable and part of being human.
- Imagine that you could allow, maybe just for a little while, that painful grievance to float up to the sky.
- Imagine that you could let go of it and set it free, like a colorful kite dancing on the wind until it is just a speck in the sky.
- What would that feel like?

Resentment blooms when we don't notice that we've come up with a set of rules for other people that they aren't interested in following or don't even know about. You don't realize that something you wished for from another person has turned into an assumption, a demand, or an expectation. You might have been seeking things from others, and now you are frustrated and hurt that these things haven't been provided to you. You may have taken an offhand remark too personally and now feel betrayed. When we harbor unexpressed or unrealistic expectations, when we don't get what we think we deserve, we are in danger of turning ourselves into victims and being trapped in corrosive and unproductive self-pity. We start asking, "Why me? I'm a good person; how could this happen to me? I don't deserve this. How could someone treat me like this?"

When we don't have the power to make things turn out the way we want, we suffer. We forget that we are often powerless over events and the reactions of other people. Why do we resist letting go of hurt even though we sense that there may be a wonderful freedom and release in letting go?

- We may cling to a resentment because we feel this is something we have power over.
- This resentment may be as comfortable and familiar as an old shirt.
- We might ask ourselves, "Is this resentment, this conflict, a stand-in for another time when I felt powerless and couldn't defend myself?"
- Are we afraid that if we let go of this resentment, we will lose something precious?
- Do we feel that if we let go of this resentment, we are betraying ourselves in some way?

If we think in a broader way, we may come to feel that we are bigger than our resentment and the other person is bigger than what we've been able to see in them. We can come to understand that we don't have to be limited or defined by the ways in which we have been hurt.

Dr. Luskin suggests that we can counter the familiar process of blame and self-pity when we do any of the following:

- Recognize we feel hurt and be gentle with ourselves
- Choose to take things less personally
- Recognize our part in a situation
- Take responsibility for our own experience and feelings
- Turn from our grievance story toward our vow, toward finding a positive intention

Where do we get stuck? What catches us? Often old, old stories from our family lives come to the surface. If we grew up in an alcoholic home, in a home where there was mental illness or physical or emotional violence, we learn to be hypervigilant, always on guard for the next danger.

We may remember mapping the number of drinks a parent would take before they became hostile. If we were teased a lot in our family, we may be hypersensitive and hypervigilant about being disrespected by others, and we may be on the lookout for insults that could be coming our way. If we lived in a house full of coldness and long silences, we may be mapping rejection everywhere, walking on eggshells, trying to make everybody happy so we don't face abandonment again. We may have inherited the hatreds and prejudices our parents fostered without thinking for ourselves. We may have grown up feeling that there wasn't enough love or attention or food to go around. That we weren't good enough. That we weren't competent or smart, that we weren't safe. These old beliefs and hurts can be triggered by small events in our everyday lives that may or may not be directed at us.

If we see the world through the map of resentment, we could be in paradise and not be satisfied. When she was growing up, my daughter and I spent our summers at Tassajara, where I would relieve the guest cooks as they went on their vacations. One day, Nova ran into a Zen priest as she walked along one of the paths in that beautiful, tranquil valley, surrounded by green leaves and the twittering of birds, by the song of the water tumbling over the rocks in the creek.

"How's it going, Nova?" he said to her.

She stopped and cocked her head. "So little time, so much to complain about."

We do have the ability to let go of our old ideas. We can understand and accept that things were the way they were, but we don't have to keep mindlessly repeating them. We can't create world peace all by ourselves. But we can work toward peace in our own lives, in our own interactions with others. We can actively cultivate our own equanimity, composure, dignity, and peace. We can recognize that each person is evolving at their own pace and time, not on our schedule. Before we speak or act, we can pause and quietly ask ourselves, "Am I going to feel good about myself if I behave in this way?" We can let go of and drop some of the armor that we have needed to protect ourselves at other times in our lives.

What is forgiveness? Fred Luskin says, "I define forgiveness as the feeling of peace you get when you take hurt less personally, take responsibility for how you feel, and become the hero instead of a victim in the story you tell." Here, I have adapted some of his suggestions about the cultivation of forgiveness:

1. In thinking about a disappointment or a resentment, allow yourself to feel it deeply throughout your body, and tell one or two trusted people about the situation and how it hurt you.

2. Make a commitment to yourself to do whatever you need to do to feel better.

3. Understand that your goal is to let go of the grievance and move on with your life. This isn't about the person who hurt you but about taking responsibility for taking care of yourself.

4. Recognize that the hurt you are feeling is something that you are allowing yourself to continue to feel by dwelling on it. You are experiencing hurt feelings, troubling thoughts, and physical reactions about something that is not happening right now.

5. When you feel upset arising, take some deep breaths and reconnect with your heart.

6. Give up expecting things from other people that they may be unwilling or unable to give you. Stop knocking on a door that won't be answered. You can work toward health, love, friendship, and prosperity, but you can't make other people or life itself give these things to you.

7. Instead of mentally replaying your hurt and resentment, try to see that there may be other ways for you to get what you need.

8. Instead of dwelling on hurts from the past and focusing on people who have hurt you, look around and find the

health, love, beauty, and friendships that are available to you now.

9. Become the hero of your story instead of the victim.

Forgiveness is the practice of extending your moments of peacefulness. Forgiveness is deciding what to pay attention to. It is the power that comes from knowing that a past injustice doesn't have to hurt today. When we have good experiences, such as moments of beauty or love, then for those moments we have forgiven those who have hurt us. Forgiveness is the choice to extend those moments to the rest of our lives. Forgiveness is available anytime. It is completely under your control. It doesn't rely on the actions of others. It is a choice you alone can make. The only way someone from the past can hurt you again is to waste this moment focusing on and reliving that betrayal.

—Fred Luskin

## Reflections and Practices

### FOCUS ON GRATITUDE

- Enjoy the feeling of your breath coming in and out of your body.
- Bring your attention to your heart by placing your hand gently on your chest.
- Feel how fortunate you are to be alive, to be able to breathe.
- Now silently say, "Thank you," on each outbreath.

- Can you bring to mind someone you would like to ask for forgiveness? It is helpful to practice first with a trusted friend. In asking for forgiveness, make sure that the emphasis is on your own behavior. Take care not to get defensive or argumentative; simply state what you would like to be forgiven for and be open to the other person telling you honestly how your behavior has affected them. Listen without judgment or interruption. Try not to be attached to a particular outcome. Thank the person for being willing to engage with you.

- Can you bring to mind someone whom you would like to forgive? This action can take place in the privacy of your own heart or in the presence of the person you would like to forgive. Before you start, make sure the other person is willing to hear you out. It will help if they have already made it clear that they would like to clear the air. Again, practicing with a close friend will be helpful. The conversation will go better if you have the intention of creating greater harmony and intimacy with this person. You might find, though, that just shifting your attitude toward someone is enough to ease tensions and that a direct conversation isn't necessary.

# 18

## The Divine Abodes

May all beings be happy,
may they be joyous and live in safety.
> —The Teaching on Loving-Kindness,
> as chanted at San Francisco Zen Center

THE BUDDHA PENETRATED the all-too-human ways that we cause suffering to ourselves and others and offered antidotes to our greed, our hatred, and our delusion.

The Buddha's teachings were transmitted orally for about four hundred years after his death and were transcribed in the first century B.C.E. by monks in Sri Lanka. Human beings have a great capacity for memorization, which we have largely abandoned. We don't even have to memorize phone numbers anymore. But when I was teaching children, my students memorized about an hour's worth of poetry. I wanted them to know that language can make us laugh, move us, teach us difficult truths. When we take words into our minds and hearts, they become a part of us. That's why it is so helpful to choose some Buddhist chants or sutras to memorize. This is a wonderful way to align ourselves with the Buddha's teachings, to bring them into our hearts, and to make a living vow.

The Buddha's oral history survived because his teachings were organized into lists, a kind of mnemonic: the Four Noble Truths, the Noble Eightfold Path, the Ten Precepts. The Four Brahmaviharas, also known as the Divine Abodes or the Four Immeasurables, offer us an alternative to the afflictive states of mind that accompany the realms of addiction. Pema Chödrön refers to these teachings as Four Kinds of Happiness. If we want to turn away from the Three Poisons—greed, hatred, and delusion—we can turn in the direction of these healing states of mind.

## The Four Brahmaviharas

The *brahmaviharas* are listed here in Pali, the language of the Buddha, with their translations:

- *Metta*—loving-kindness
- *Karuna*—compassion
- *Mudita*—sympathetic joy
- *Upekkha*—equanimity

When I was about eighteen years old, I was walking across the campus at San Francisco State, and a social science major with a clipboard stopped me and asked, "What do you want out of life?" To my surprise, without skipping a beat, I said, "Equanimity." Little did I know that, to find that elusive equanimity, I would need to arrest my alcoholism through the work of recovery, and I would need to find and practice the Buddha's Middle Way.

It isn't clear to me whether we attain equanimity by cultivating loving-kindness, compassion, and sympathetic joy, or whether those three capacities flow out of our equanimity. Perhaps they are like a Möbius strip, a kind of continuity that we can reflect on.

---

Metta, or loving-kindness, is characterized as wholehearted friendliness toward the whole world. We are so accustomed to dividing the world up into what we like, what we don't like, and what we feel neutral toward, that we are probably largely unconscious of this constant process of leaning toward or away from things and people. Of grasping at what we want and pushing away what we dislike. If we can keep loving-kindness in mind, if we can cultivate unlimited friendliness and approach the world this way, giving the world the benefit of the doubt and extending ourselves out to others, we will see a marvelous transformation in our lives.

One way I practice this is by thanking everyone. I thank the mail delivery person for their service. I thank the gardeners in Golden Gate Park for taking care of it for all of us. My heart sinks a bit when I see someone talking on their cell phone while someone else is checking out and bagging their groceries for them. It feels so much better to look the people who are helping us in the eye and exchange a few words and a little warmth and humanity with one another.

We are all so busy getting to the next thing that we don't always take time to be kind to the person right in front of us. One of my third graders said, "It's a lot more fun to be kind than it is to be mean."

I often see people sitting in their cars with their engines running, hypnotized by their cell phones as they pollute the environment and squander fossil fuels. This unconscious behavior is a metaphor for our lack of alignment toward others and our lack of gratitude for our precious earth's resources.

Recently, there have been many studies on the brain and happiness. We have learned more about the brain in the last twenty years than we've ever known before. Elsewhere, I've mentioned habits that have been found to be both beneficial to our brain function and to the cultivation of happiness:

- Having strong social connections with others
- Getting physical exercise
- Spending time in nature
- Finding meaning and purpose in work
- Exploring our creativity
- Bringing novelty into our lives by trying new things
- Meditating, especially on loving-kindness
- Focusing on gratitude

The Metta Sutta, or Teaching on Loving-Kindness, can be found in the back of the book. This chant includes a phrase that I call to mind when I find myself spiraling downward in my thinking. It is easy to lapse into a downward spiral when we contemplate the seemingly irrevocable deep divides in our country, the effects of global warming, the violence breaking out around the world, the devastating impacts of the pandemic. When I hear a siren, when I think of a friend who is in distress, when I find myself indulging in negative thoughts about someone, when I get on the hamster wheel of obsessive worry, I call this phrase to mind:

May all beings be happy,
May they be joyous and live in safety.

I chant the Metta Sutta every day and know it by heart. When I have trouble sleeping or find myself waiting in line, I can recite it to myself to renew my vow to live in loving-kindness every day.

We can hold in our hearts our intention to extend unlimited friendliness toward the whole world, but at the same time, there may be people or situations that call for caution. We have to trust our gut here, and if something or someone sends up red flags, we should honor our inmost wisdom. If we grew up with mental illness, alcoholism, violence, homophobia, racism, or misogyny, we probably needed coping skills that protected us from harm. We may have felt that we had to protect ourselves because no one else would. We may have developed "street smarts" that alerted us to danger. We may have learned the magical ability of becoming completely invisible. Remembered trauma can also make us hypervigilant. Now, as adults, we can make reasonable decisions about when we can allow ourselves to show more vulnerability.

In recovery, as we loosen the tight grip of self-centered fear and the greed, hatred, and delusion that are at the heart of addiction, we begin to feel a new openness and loving-kindness toward the whole world.

------

Compassion, or karuna, literally means to share someone else's pain, to suffer with them. This isn't the same thing as feeling sorry for someone. This is recognizing our mutual humanity, the human suffering that is inevitable as long as we live in a human body.

There was a wonderful elder statesman in the recovery community in San Francisco—I will call him Ed—who helped countless others recover from alcoholism. Ed was working in his garage at home when a fire started, and he was rushed to the hospital with painful burns.

A nurse there, who was in recovery herself, said to him, "You know, Ed, there's a young man here who was in a motorcycle accident, and he is in the same kind of pain you are coping with. He's a recovering alcoholic, and it would really help him if you could meet with him."

In sharing this story, Ed said that, during the time he sat talking with that other suffering man, he was relieved of his excruciating pain for a time.

Years later, Ed ran into that motorcycle rider at a meeting in Sacramento, and the younger man told him, "You know, when we were both in the hospital, a nurse there told me, 'There's an older man here who is in recovery, and it would be really helpful to him if you would meet and talk with him.'" Clearly, that wise nurse understood the healing power of compassion.

We can't access compassion for others until we can have compassion for ourselves. Part of our work in recovery is to retrieve our self-esteem and sense of purpose. As we help others, we forgive ourselves for our past mistakes and for the dangerous detours we had to take to find our way here. The compassion we feel for one another in recovery is rich and deep because we've all been there ourselves. And we find compassion for all beings when we recognize our deep interconnectedness.

---

Compassion is the ability to share in the sorrows of others. Sympathetic joy is the ability to share in their joys. This isn't always as easy as we might think. There is an evocative word in German, *schadenfreude*, which means "deriving joy from the misfortunes of others." Sympathetic joy is the opposite of this. When something wonderful happens to someone else, we wish them well and support them in their happiness. In recovery, when someone reaches a milestone, we clap and cheer for them because we are now capable of feeling sympathetic joy. Our own recovery is renewed and deepened by their success.

In our greed, hatred, and delusion, we may secretly rejoice when someone who has wronged us suffers. We may begrudge them any kind of happiness or ease. But the realm of resentment and vindictiveness isn't a pleasant place to be. The physical effect of holding on to anger and resentment is well known; in clinging to these shrinking emotions, we harm ourselves as well as others. In our recovery programs, we learn how corrosive and dangerous resentment and self-pity are, indulgences that can lead us back to the substance or behavior that we abused. Self-righteous anger isn't for us.

---

Equanimity is simply coming back to center. The excessive highs and lows of addiction have mellowed, and no longer numb, we appreciate the quiet joys of everyday life. If we can cultivate loving-kindness, compassion, and sympathetic joy, equanimity will follow. If we cultivate equanimity, coming back to our breath, coming back to our center again and again, loving-kindness, compassion, and sympathetic joy will arise as well.

In Zen we don't sit with any idea of gain; we don't sit to improve ourselves or get anywhere in particular. We sit in silence, putting aside for a time our narrow and limiting ideas about ourselves and the world, returning to the breath and experiencing a wonderful expansiveness. If we practice in this way, the Four Brahmaviharas are within reach.

## Reflections and Practices

- Sit quietly in your zazen posture for a few minutes, coming back to your breath.
- One way to cultivate these healing states is simply to call them to mind. Choose one of these qualities and allow it flow through you as you live your everyday life. If you turn toward the term *loving-kindness* during the day, you might let someone go ahead of you in line or in traffic. You might smile at a stranger. You might act on a generous impulse. You might refrain from an unkind comment. You might tell your partner how much you appreciate them or send a loving note to a friend who is far away.
- In your zazen posture, bring to mind someone to whom you are close. Visualize their beloved face, and imagine a golden glow around them. Let them hover there in your mind and body and send them this wish: "May _____ be happy, may they be joyous and live in safety." You can enact this same practice with someone to whom you feel

neutral. When you are feeling grounded, you can also practice this with someone with whom you are in conflict. Of course, it is invaluable to bring this same loving awareness to ourselves, wishing for our own safety, joy, and happiness.

• Thank everyone.

# AFTERWORD

After the election on November 8, 2016, we gathered in the music room at The San Francisco School as Doug Goodkin, a legendary music teacher, led the students in a song about a gray goose, and we joined in on the chorus. It's an African American song about a goose that, despite others' repeated efforts to destroy her, survives and flies deep into the sky, a long string of goslings behind her. I wondered why Doug had chosen that song for this occasion, but when we finished, he said that each of us has a gray goose within us that can take flight and free us. No one can touch it; no one can take it away from us. There is a place inside each of us that is sacred and inviolable. No matter what happens in the world, no matter how dark the times, the bright wings of freedom are within each of us.

Doug said to the children, "You may not understand it completely now, but someday you will know that today is an important day in our country's history, a day when many of the values this school stands for are in danger—democracy, social justice, personal responsibility, the beauty and power of diversity. And later, when you do understand, I want you to look back and remember that on this day, at our school, we gathered, and we sang."

Recovery is about freedom, that flight of freedom within us that no one can take away unless we allow them to. Freedom from the craving that we hoped would soothe us and help us forget ourselves for a while. Freedom from the regret, the shame, and the guilt that accompany addiction. Today, I share my life with my partner, David. I wake up in the morning, grateful for another day of practice and recovery, and before I go to sleep, I give thanks. I celebrate my daughter, Nova, and the journey that she has taken to become a gifted teacher of children and a warrior for social justice. My friends, my family, all those who walk this path of practice and recovery, I couldn't have gotten from *there* to *here* without you.

There are both sudden and gradual awakenings in practice and recovery. Once, when I was stepping out of the zendo at Tassajara, the entire shimmering world suddenly awakened with me in that moment. When I had been sober for about three years, I woke up and something was different. I realized that, gradually, my shame had slipped away. There is an image in Zen of a monk who walks outside into a light rain, and when he returns, his robes are damp. This speaks of the subtle, yet cataclysmic, effect of practice transforming our lives.

With the clarity of practice and recovery, we can wake up to the world and to one another with a full heart and clear eyes. We can say to anyone, anytime, "Don't worry. I know who I am."

May the longtime sun shine upon you,
All love surround you,
And the pure light within you
Guide your way on.

—Scottish blessing

# VOICES FROM RECOVERY

People on different paths share their stories of practice and recovery:

> I returned to Zen practice after many years away—years that included heroin addiction and recovery, followed by years of sober living without any formal practice. Within a practice context, I found I was ashamed of my addiction and had difficulty reconciling it with the years of monastic practice that preceded it. How could I have any experience or understanding of Buddhism and still have given in to addiction? But I came to realize that Buddha-nature does not exclude anything. This addicted/recovered being is the perfect buddha. There is no other. As Dogen Zenji tells us, "Those who regard mundane life as an obstacle to the buddha-dharma, know only that there is no buddha-dharma in the mundane life, they do not yet know that there is no mundane life in the buddha-dharma." ("Bendowa," *Shobogenzo*) There is no other place to practice, no other place to find realization, but in this very life in which each of us are living.
>
> —Deborah

> I am an Al-Anon dropout. But I remember and appreciate the wisdom of the Serenity Prayer, as well as the 12 Steps. My

son, my qualifier, has been clean and sober since he entered rehab almost two and a half years ago. I don't delude myself about what the future could hold, but for the time being, he is doing well in many aspects of his life. For now, my praying centers around Taoist teachings, my oneness with the universe, and the active collection of qi essence inside myself. My daily, or almost daily, Buddhist meditation also brings me a new sense of peace.

—Karen

In January 1995, when I was fourteen years sober, we were chanting the Sixteen Bodhisattva Precepts during the monthly full moon ceremony at the Zen Center. I heard myself say, "I vow not to intoxicate mind or body of self or others," and I barely heard the rest.

This precept is saying that it is much bigger than not drinking alcohol or using drugs; it includes our mind states and what comes out of our mouths. I thought, "I've been physically sober for a while, but I've intoxicated my mind and the minds of others." I had never thought about it like that. The Zen priest Reb Anderson, in his book *Being Upright*, says, "The precept of not intoxicating mind or body of self or others is for all of us who have difficulty remaining upright in the midst of our suffering. It encourages us to trust being upright, instead of using intoxicants, as the best way to deal with our restlessness, anxiety, and pain." That, to me, says that staying sober is being upright, and it is our best chance, maybe our only chance, of dealing with our sometimes restless, irritable, and discontented lives.

—Judith

I began my recovery from alcoholism at age sixty-five. At that time, the trajectory of my life was not focused on career, a significant other, and worldly achievement, but more on inner house cleaning, interpersonal connection, and spiritual development. The 12 Steps of AA, especially the fourth and fifth steps, revealed parts of myself that were previously hidden. I learned to accept that to be human was to be imperfect. My imperfections were not shameful but connected me to others, and I found I could be less of what I thought others wanted me to be. Other alcoholics told stories with honesty and vulnerability, and this inspired me to accept what I could not change and to begin to change what I could. My spiritual journey before AA was marked by spiritual bypass. I thought that somehow spiritual practice would allow me to transcend my pain and shortcomings, something like the relief I felt when drinking. In AA, I found that, to walk on a spiritual path, I had to become more fully human.

—John

I am a woman, a person in recovery, a Buddhist, a filmmaker. And I am a teller of stories. My latest documentary follows nine artists in recovery from addictive behaviors who are transformed by creativity in their search for freedom. During the making of the film, I was challenged to go deeper into investigating my own recovery and Buddhist practices.

A hip-hop artist in the film who I call "Justin" gained popularity rapping about his recovery. We had videos of him performing but wanted to see spontaneous recordings of his daily life and recovery story, so we sent him a cell phone. As the videos came in, we were inspired by his willingness to be vulnerable in front of a camera.

But over time it became more and more difficult to get in touch with Justin, and we watched helplessly as his addiction took hold again. Witnessing him using drugs during a video shoot, I was filled with anxiety. My old energy habit of compulsively wanting to rush in and fix the addicts in my life whom I love resurfaced with a vengeance. What could I do to change him? I wanted to "fix" him, for his recovery to get back on track, and for things in the moment to be different than they were.

I remembered the Al-Anon wisdom that I didn't cause his addiction and that I cannot control or cure him. What I can do in this situation is reach for my Buddhist practice and set my attention to be a steady presence for myself. I could hold space for myself and become willing to accept my own experience, beginning with counting my breath. By turning my attention toward this unwanted experience in the present, something new became possible. I am not alone; I am supported by my Al-Anon groups and the Buddhist sangha. I continue to reach out to Justin, who has disappeared into the streets, his cell phone lost or sold for drugs. I don't know what is in store for Justin, but I can practice compassion for him and all addicts out there on the streets. May all beings live in peace and be free from suffering.

—Dianne

The eleventh step reads, "Sought through prayer and meditation to improve our conscious contact with God, as we understood him, praying only for knowledge of His will for us and the power to carry that out." For years I have struggled with this important maintenance step of the 12-Step program. The biggest struggle was slowing down and developing the self-discipline to take the time to do it daily. I read many books on practice, went to workshops, gained knowledge, and still could not develop a daily mindfulness practice. A friend of mine once said to me that I like to *think* of myself as someone who *would* meditate!

Sixteen years ago, I was invited to go to a hot yoga class. That experience was the beginning of a love relationship I have with the practice of yoga. I have a devotion to it that I have not experienced with other forms of practice. I was relieved to learn, during a conversation with my sponsor, that yoga and other forms of moving meditation count. Having experienced the joys and benefits of mindfulness through movement, it is now a comfort to sit quietly and breathe.

—Susan L.

I got sober when I was sixteen. I know that sounds young, but I started drinking and using drugs when I was twelve to stop the pain in my head. It worked at first, and I had a lot of fun with my friends, but it didn't take long for me to see that I was a "real" alcoholic. It helped that my dad got sober a long time ago, so I had that example. He knew I needed AA, but he knew that I had to find it on my own. AA saved my life. I'm twenty-one now. I have lost friends to this disease. But I'm glad I have sober friends, and we help each other. I'm just learning about Zen and meditation and that helps too.

—Danny

I struggled with addiction for twenty years, and now I've been depression-free for more than thirty. I think depression is a kind of addiction: it's an addiction to negative thinking. Even though it feels like you are a victim of your negative thoughts and circumstances, you are the one that's thinking them, characterizing them. These negative thought patterns have become ingrained and instead of realizing that they are a choice, they have become a belief. Just because you believe something does not make it true. To get out of depression, you need to doubt your own beliefs and go back to a nonjudgmental blank slate. To me it feels like water in a ditch; once you have a ditch, that's where the water will flow, or thoughts, in this case. I had so many negative thoughts about myself, no matter what others thought and said about me, it was what I believed to be true. To turn away from the habit of depression, you have to dig new ditches.

—Barbara

I started getting in trouble with drugs and alcohol when I was in middle school. By the time I was in high school, I was doing things that didn't make me feel good about myself. A school counselor didn't judge me or report me, but she told me that AA might help. I still don't know where I found the strength to find a meeting, but I was surprised when I got there that there were a few other people my age. I got a sponsor, and she helped me work the steps and gave me the book *Zen Mind, Beginner's Mind*. Having a sitting practice and learning about Buddhism have helped me stay present and find my true center. Today, I am twenty-three and grateful for the gift of sobriety. Sharing this program with other young women who are like me makes me so happy!

—R.B.

I know people don't think that men have eating disorders, but I did. Because of childhood trauma, I didn't want to be alive, so there were times when I wouldn't eat. This also helped me get the attention I craved. When I found recovery, I found out that I want to live. Today, I practice the principles of recovery, and that has helped me have a better relationship around food. I am a member of a Buddhist sangha that supports me, along with my recovery fellowship. I can't think of a better way of life.

—D. F.

I started drinking in my teens because it seemed fun and miraculously offered an escape from my self-hatred and shyness. As an adult I was a "high-functioning" alcoholic, although I didn't realize it until my fifties, when I wanted to drink "less," shamefully hiding all those bottles, but found I could not stop the craving for a drink. I woke up and made a call to my hospital's substance abuse program. It seems hard to believe, but just asking for help was the day I totally stopped drinking up until today, which is sixteen years later. I learned in a recovery program the many reasons *why* one drinks, but it is the sharing with other alcoholics, both giving and hearing our stories and feelings, that has given me the *how* of staying sober. I'm keeping on the learning path to self-acceptance and being here now.

—J.P.

Swimming in the rivers of life,
it's too hard to keep treading water alone.
The practices of Buddhism and Recovery
create a great raft for me.
Navigating together in community with
my Zen Center Sangha and Al-Anon/AA family,
support and friendship are here.
I just have to keep getting in the boat.
Oh, Great Ocean,
thank you for this life.

—Sam


In Soto Zen, a *sesshin*—literally "touching the heart-mind"—
is a period of intensive zazen in a Zen monastery. I joined a
practice period at San Francisco Zen Center's Green Gulch
Farm in January 1995, not realizing what I was in for. At the
end of January, our small group was told we would have our
first five-day sesshin, sitting silently in the zendo for forty-
minute periods all day long. The night before it started, our
group was brought together for what they call "the admoni-
tions." The admonitions before a sesshin are, "No reading,
no writing, and no speaking for five days." No reading? I
was fourteen years sober at the time, and on my first AA
birthday a friend had given me a little daily meditation book
for women in recovery called *Each Day a New Beginning* by
Karen Casey. I read it every morning. Eijun Linda Cutts, a
Zen priest, gave us the admonitions, and afterward I asked
if I could talk to her. I told her that I read the daily writ-

ing in this little recovery book every day. She thought for a moment and suggested I memorize something from it and say it to myself each day. Back in my room, I looked at that day's reading and then for some reason went back to January 1. It said, "Our higher power is as close as our breath. Conscious awareness of its presence strengthens us, moment by moment. The past is gone. Today is full of possibilities. With each breath I will be aware of the strength at hand."

It was so perfect. I memorized it that night, and the next morning, just as we started the first period of zazen, I said it to myself. I've been saying it ever since.

—J.K.

I really appreciate practicing with the Brahmaviharas and thinking of them as the path of happiness. One of the traps for me is imagining I don't deserve to be happy, that I don't deserve to enjoy my life fully when there is so much suffering around me. It was so valuable to learn in Al-Anon to stand in my own experience, to recognize I could enjoy my life without guilt even if my children were struggling, my husband was depressed, my father was drinking. So freeing.

During this pandemic time, I sometimes felt myself getting caught up again, this time in the woes of the world. With the recent death of Archbishop Desmond Tutu, I went back to revisit *The Book of Joy*. His words deeply encourage me: "It helps no one if you sacrifice your joy because others are suffering. We people who care must be attractive, must be filled with joy, so that others recognize that caring, that helping and being generous are not a burden, they are a joy.

Give the world your love, your service, your healing, but you can also give your joy. This, too, is a great gift."

—Denise

I stopped drinking alcohol several years before I first uttered the words, "I am an alcoholic." In recovery terms, I was a dry drunk. Stubborn and white-knuckled, it took me a long time before I could claim alcoholism as one of my issues.

I came to my first 12-Step meeting to support a friend, certain in my codependency that I could save her. In that first meeting, other alcoholics shared their truths so fearlessly, and without any semblance of shame, that I had a spiritual awakening simply by sitting in those chairs. It was their willingness to speak their truths so freely that enthralled me.

I wanted that freedom. A week later, I spoke the truth of my own disease for the first time: "My name is Éanlaí, and I am an alcoholic." As a trauma survivor, those simple words knocked loose some profound shame I had carried with me since childhood. A shame I had imbibed from the man who abused me, a shame I had carried for decades as my own. Alcohol, my self-prescribed antidote, the thing that initially set me free, had eventually accelerated the flames of my self-hatred into something uncontrollable.

Not until I took the first step—*We admitted we were powerless over alcohol, that our lives had become unmanageable*—did I turn toward something I had not yet fully claimed: the power to choose. Truly choose. It seems to be a miracle of contradiction that, by admitting my powerlessness over alcohol, I found not helplessness but choice. The power to decide for myself rather than be driven. The power to choose a new way of life. A new outlook and set of principles to mitigate the old shames, to make of them an unshakable new foundation, step by step.

This year, I handed the name of the man who abused me in childhood over to the police. And in so doing, I gave back the shame with which I had been burdened to its rightful owner, the shame he had so freely given to me. A gargantuan task made possible by recovery. I did not do this alone. The "we" of recovery, and the "easy does it, but do it" philosophy of gradual psychic shifts, helped me transform the hapless victim of my past into the hope-filled, sober woman of my present. And indeed, my future. One among many.

—E.C.

I have been drawn to the notion of some kind of spirituality ever since I first read *Be Here Now* by Baba Ram Dass and *Siddhartha* by Hermann Hesse, back in the seventies. Both books had a big impact on me. I started reading books about Zen Buddhism when my drinking was taking off, but every time I got to the part in a particular book that talked about meditation, I would put the book down. I thought I had to stop thinking to meditate properly, to do it *right*, and I knew I couldn't stop my rabid brain. That's why I drank.

It was a watershed moment for me when I learned you don't have to stop your brain from thinking. You can't; it's what the brain does. For me, practicing meditation is a way to have a different relationship with my thinking, as is working the 12 Steps. I can notice my thoughts, so many tired loops on repeat, and I can let them slip past, like watching a river go by. Coming back to my breath again and again. That's all. I am still pretty sure everyone is doing it better than I am, but even that thought is recognizable now, and I can note it and drop it, or I can get on the train for a ride.

—P.C.

I was in trouble with gambling long before I admitted it and walked into a Gamblers Anonymous meeting. I can't even tell you how much I lost and how much I hurt my family. Being a gambler didn't fit with how other people saw me, so I lived that double life of the addict. But I was always lonely, chasing that high. Today my friends in recovery and the members of my sangha really care about me and help me be my best self. Luckily, I have my family back. I will never get over this disease, but each day I feel stronger and more committed to my practice and to my recovery. I never want to go back to that dark place again.

—Mike L.

# CHANTS FROM SAN FRANCISCO ZEN CENTER

## Metta Sutta: Teaching on Loving-Kindness

This is what should be accomplished by the one who is
    wise,
who seeks the good, and has obtained peace:

Let one be strenuous, upright and sincere,
without pride, easily contented and joyous.
Let one not be submerged by the things of the world.
Let one not take upon oneself the burden of riches.
Let one's senses be controlled.
Let one be wise but not puffed up,
and let one not desire great possessions,
even for one's family.
Let one do nothing that is mean or that the wise would
    reprove.

May all beings be happy,
may they be joyous and live in safety.

All living beings, whether weak or strong,
in high or middle or low realms of existence,
small or great, visible or invisible, near or far,
born or to be born, may all beings be happy.

Let no one deceive another nor despise any being in any
    state.
Let none by anger or hatred wish harm to another.

Even as a mother, at the risk of her life,
watches over and protects her only child,
so with a boundless mind should one cherish all living
    things,
suffusing love over the entire world,
above, below, and all around without limit.

So let one cultivate an infinite goodwill toward the whole
    world.
Standing or walking, sitting or lying down, during all
    one's waking hours
let one practice the way with gratitude.
Not holding to fixed views, endowed with insight, freed
    from sense appetites,
one who achieves the way will be freed from the duality
    of birth and death.

## Meal Chant

Innumerable labors brought us this food.
We should know how it comes to us.

Receiving this offering, we should consider
Whether our virtue and practice deserve it.
Desiring the natural order of mind,
We should be free from greed, hate, and delusion.
We eat to support life and to practice the way of Buddha.

This food is for the Three Treasures,
for our teachers, family, and all people,
and for all beings in the six worlds.

The first portion is to avoid all evil.
The second is to do all good.
The third is to save all beings.
Thus we eat this food and awaken with everyone.


## Homage to the Perfection of Wisdom

Homage to the perfection of wisdom, the lovely, the holy.
The perfection of wisdom gives light.
Unstained, the entire world cannot stain her.
She is a source of light, and from everyone in the triple
    worlds,
she removes darkness.
Most excellent are her works.
She brings light
so that all fear and distress may be forsaken,
and disperses the gloom and darkness of delusion.
She herself is an organ of vision.
She has a clear knowledge
of the own-being of all dharmas

for she does not stray away from it.
The perfection of wisdom of the buddhas
Sets in motion the Wheel of Dharma.

# THE SIXTEEN BODHISATTVA

# PRECEPTS

## The Refuges

I take refuge in Buddha.
I take refuge in Dharma.
I take refuge in Sangha.

## The Three Pure Precepts

I vow to refrain from all evil.
I vow to make every effort to live in enlightenment.
I vow to live and be lived for the benefit of all beings.

## The Ten Grave Precepts

I vow not to kill.
I vow not to take what is not given.
I vow not to misuse sexuality.
I vow to refrain from false speech.
I vow not to intoxicate the mind or body of self or others.
I vow not to slander others.
I vow not to praise self at the expense of others.

I vow not to be avaricious.
I vow not to harbor ill will.
I vow not to abuse the Three Treasures.

# ACKNOWLEDGMENTS

I thank the circles of community that have sustained my practice and recovery for many years: my family and my lifelong friends; my companions on the path of recovery; my dharma friends at Zen Center and beyond; the hundreds of children I have taught at Alvarado Elementary School and The San Francisco School, as well as their parents and my colleagues; The Trees; and the Lenox House Meditation and Recovery group in Oakland. I thank Ivan Bercholz and Shambhala Publications for fostering my work, Beth Frankl and Samantha Ripley for their wise guidance with *The Zen Way of Recovery*, and Karen Steib for her thoughtful editing. I thank my daughter, Nova, and my partner, David, for their love and support.

This book began to take shape during my sojourn at Dorland Mountain Arts Colony, where I was given the time and space to begin.

I am grateful that I have been able to practice for many years at the three practice places of San Francisco Zen Center: City Center, Green Gulch Farm, and Tassajara Zen Mountain Center. I treasure my teacher, Eijun Linda Ruth Cutts, and her deep devotion to this practice.

I am especially thankful for my years at Tassajara, located east of Big Sur, California, in the Los Padres Wilderness. During the summer, Tassajara is open for the guest season, and the rest of the year it functions as a place for people to practice and train in Zen Buddhism. Students live in cabins clustered around the zendo, or meditation hall, where they sit zazen and engage in services and ceremonies. Very early in the morning, a monk holding a wooden hammer hits a big wooden slab that hangs outside the zendo. This is called the *han*, and it calls the monks to the meditation hall. This haiku was written by my brother when he visited Tassajara:

TASSAJARA HAN
Hardwood cleaves a dream.
Full moon in the western sky,
Flashlight left behind.

—Peter Cameron

# SUGGESTED READINGS

*Beyond Happiness: The Zen Way to True Contentment* by Ezra Bayda (Boulder, CO: Shambhala Publications, 2010).

*The Compass of Pleasure: How Our Brains Make Fatty Foods, Orgasm, Exercise, Marijuana, Generosity, Vodka, Learning, and Gambling Feel So Good* by David Linden (New York: Penguin Books, 2012).

*The Dhammapada*, a collection of the Buddha's teachings. Many different translations are available.

*Fixing My Gaze: A Scientist's Journey into Seeing in Three Dimensions* by Susan R. Barry (New York: Basic Books, 2010).

*Forgive for Good: A Proven Prescription for Health and Happiness* by Fred Luskin (San Francisco: HarperSanFrancisco, 2002).

*Happiness: A Guide to Developing Life's Most Important Skill* by Matthieu Ricard (New York: Little, Brown and Company, 2006).

*The Heart of Buddha's Teaching: Transforming Suffering into Peace, Joy, and Liberation* by Thich Nhat Hanh (New York: Harmony Books, 2015).

*The Hidden Lamp: Stories from Twenty-Five Centuries of Awakened Women*, edited by Florence Caplow and Susan Moon (Somerville, MA: Wisdom Publications, 2013).

*In the Realm of Hungry Ghosts: Close Encounters with Addiction* by Gabor Mate (Berkeley, CA: North Atlantic Books, 2020).

*Not Always So: Practicing the True Spirit of Zen* by Shunryu Suzuki Roshi, edited by Edward Espe Brown (New York: HarperCollins, 2002).

*On Death and Dying: What the Dying Have to Teach Doctors, Nurse, Clergy, and Their Own Families* by Elisabeth Kübler-Ross (Fiftieth Anniversary Edition. New York: Scribner, 2014).

*One Breath at a Time: Buddhism and the Twelve Steps* by Kevin Griffin (Emmaus, PA: Rodale, 2004).

*Opening the Hand of Thought: Foundations of Zen Buddhist Practice* by Kosho Uchiyama, translated and edited by Tom Wright, Jisho Warner, and Shohaku Okumura (Somerville, MA: Wisdom Publications, 2004).

*Radical Acceptance: Embracing Your Life with the Heart of a Buddha* by Tara Brach (New York: Bantam Books, 2003).

*Radical Compassion: Learning to Love Yourself and Your World with the Practice of RAIN* by Tara Brach (New York: Viking, 2019).

*Taking Our Places: The Buddhist Path to Truly Growing Up* by Norman Fisher (San Francisco: HarperCollins, 2003).

*Twelve Steps on Buddha's Path: Bill, Buddha, and We* by Laura S. (Somerville, MA: Wisdom Publications, 2006).

*Varieties of Religious Experience* by William James (New York: Library of America Paperback Classics, 2010).

*When Things Fall Apart: Heart Advice for Difficult Times* by Pema Chödrön (Boulder, CO: Shambhala Publications, 1997), as well as other books by Pema Chödrön.

*Zen Mind, Beginner's Mind* by Shunryu Suzuki Roshi (Boulder, CO: Shambhala Publications, 2011).

## To introduce children to Buddhism

*Buddhist Stories for Kids: Jataka Tales of Kindness, Friendship and Forgiveness* by Laura Burges (Boulder, CO: Bala Kids, 2023).

*Zen for Kids: 50+ Mindful Activities and Stories to Shine Loving Kindness in the World* by Laura Burges (Boulder, CO: Bala Kids, 2023).

For additional addiction resources, see the National Council on Alcoholism and Drug Dependence: https://ncadd.us.